the

1906–2006
SOUL WINNING
CENTURY...

the SOUL WINNING CENTURY...
1906–2006

The Humbard Family Legacy...One Hundred Years of Ministry

REX HUMBARD

CLARION CALL MARKETING

DALLAS, TEXAS

THE SOUL-WINNING CENTURY

© 2006 Clarion Call Marketing

Published by Clarion Call Marketing
P.O. Box 610010
Dallas, TX 75261

ISBN 1-59574-055-4

Printed in the United States of America

2006—First Edition

10 9 8 7 6 5 4 3 2 1

CONTENTS

FOREWORD

I have heard, seen, and read about Rex Humbard for as long as I have been a Christian. And I have been privileged to be a friend to Rex and Maude Aimee for a number of years. Every time I sit with this precious couple in their living room or spend time with them on the *This Is Your Day!* studio set or stand with them on a crusade stage, I am reminded of the tremendous history and soul-winning legacy they embody.

I am often asked by people, "How can I get into full-time ministry?" This book helps provide the answer. Rex Humbard's life is a great example of how a young lad pursued God's will, added to the legacy his father founded, walked through open doors, kept on keeping on, and even now, as this book attests, remains steadfast in his desire to reach souls for Jesus Christ.

As you read the chapters of this remarkable book, you will realize, more than ever, what a blessing Rex and Maude Aimee are to the body of Christ. You will also get to witness the history of evangelism during the twentieth century and take the journey of a lifetime with these pioneers of the faith!

Thank you, Rex and Maude Aimee, for blazing the trail. May the flames of faith that you started continue to spread all over the world until the glorious return of our wonderful Lord Jesus. Only then will we know how vast are the multitudes of men, women, boys, and girls whose lives were brought to the foot of Calvary's cross through the ministry of the Humbard family!

—BENNY HINN
World Healing Center Church

PREFACE

In a cluttered house trailer sat an aging, bewhiskered old man, smoking a corncob pipe, drinking hard liquor, and muttering curses. He had spent his life as a classic scoundrel—a wanton womanizer, a debt-jumper—abusing his longsuffering wife and alienating his numerous children.

His only link to redemption was a flickering image on an ancient black-and-white television set. Every Sunday morning, the old man went to church by tuning in to a certain television show.

"That Rex," the old man rasped, "he's my pastor."

Year after year, through that weekly program, the truth of the Word seeped into the old man's heart. Finally one day, after more than a decade under the ministry of "that Rex," the old man finally accepted Christ as his Savior.

Within a few weeks, he died and was received into the arms of Jesus.

That crusty old "sinner saved by grace" was my grandfather.

So there was a certain pleasing irony for me to go to work for Rex Humbard.

I was a skinny twenty-year-old nail-biter, desperately ambitious but also terribly insecure, when Rex took me in and made something of me.

One of my former pastors asked Rex to hire me as a writer-editor in the Humbard ministry's publications area. Rex said yes, but not on the basis of my schooling (minimal), my experience (even less), or my spiritual depth (questionable). He was interested in creativity, passion, and hard work: Would this kid come up with new ways to do the old job of reaching lost souls with the Gospel? Would this kid sell out to the cause of reaching lost souls with the Gospel? Would this kid stay up all night for the sake of reaching lost souls with the Gospel?

Rex didn't care about anything else.

To go to work at the Rex Humbard Ministry was like stepping into an enormous jet engine. This phenomenal force was sucking in every possible resource—every high-potential worker, every available dollar, every workable strategy, every new idea—and focusing all this energy in one direction, driving directly forward with the greatest possible power. One day Rex and his leadership team came up with an idea for a book. I went to my little apartment and started banging on an old typewriter (those were the days before PCs), writing almost literally around the clock. And just nine days after the idea was hatched, tens of thousands of books came off the press! In moments like these, which were many, I could only sit with my mouth hanging open, shaking my head in awe. Rex and Company routinely worked miracles, because no idea was too far-fetched if it meant reaching more souls for Christ.

Yet on a personal level, Rex was quite unlike the incredible ministry machine that had grown up around him. He was quiet and unassuming, modest and humble. I was foolish in many ways and must have often been enormously annoying, but Rex was unfailingly polite.

His heart was great and true. One afternoon before yet another massive evangelistic crusade in some far-flung city, I was outdoors and happened to look across a wide plaza to notice Rex walking alone. He had no entourage, no bodyguards. Presently, a woman emerged from the crowd, and I saw Rex stop to respond to her. She clearly knew him from television. I began making my way through the crowd, figuring I might rescue Rex from a bothersome fan. But before I could get to them, I saw Rex take both her hands and bow his head. The woman lowered her face and began to weep as Rex prayed fervently for her, unashamedly, in the middle of a public square, with crowds milling around. I remember my shock, realizing for the first time that Rex was not only about multitudes of souls, he was about *each* soul.

It was my privilege to write many, many column inches of *The Answer* magazine and to work over the years on numerous books for the ministry, from *Billy Wasn't There* to *The Rex Humbard Prophecy Bible*. It's probably safe to say that I touched more lives through Rex's ministry than in all my subsequent years as a pastor, author, and dramatist.

When I married, Rex did me the great kindness of traveling to my home in Phoenix, Arizona, and officiating at the ceremony. In the years that followed, after I became a teaching pastor, I occasionally preached Rex's own sermons (with his blessing). And it perhaps closes the circle—from my grandfather's salvation, to my "initiation" as Rex's writer and editor, to my wedding—to have worked with Rex on this, his autobiography. To be invited to serve on this project was one of the greatest honors of my life.

Sitting next to Rex in his study, poring over old texts and photographs, rolling tape on his recollections, I couldn't help but look him over. His hair is white; he has the rice-paper skin of an old man. When he gets up to find a certain book on the shelf, his steps are cautious. But no matter the topic of conversation, before many moments have passed, he comes back around to the subject of souls. And that's when his eyes flash like the eyes of a young fighter. He lights up. His back straightens. His fingers move fluidly. He is what God clearly created him to be, and that calling knows no limitations.

Rex has certainly broken through all the boundaries for the cause of Christ, and it has been a joy to journey with him.

—Doug Brendel
Scottsdale, Arizona

INTRODUCTION

Committed for Life

*I*f I live to be a hundred—and that day is fast approaching—I will still be about one thing: winning lost souls to Jesus Christ.

I have been about evangelism from my childhood. My father, Alpha Humbard, was about evangelism from his youth. My own wife and children and grandchildren have worked with me in evangelism for decades. My father, born in 1890, came to faith in Christ at sixteen, when Theodore Roosevelt was president. My father did not wait to finish high school; he did not go to seminary. He was instantly and unstoppably passionate about winning souls to Christ, so he began in evangelistic ministry immediately, and he never stopped. I came to Christ as a small boy, caught a vision of the difference between heaven and hell, and began serving alongside my father when I was still very young. I have never stopped either, and 2006 will be the one hundredth anniversary of continuous Humbard evangelism ministry.

I share all this, not to glorify myself or the Humbard name, but to point again, as always, to Jesus Christ. Our family's dogged commitment

1

to evangelism grows out of the fact that nothing is more important in this life than knowing and accepting Jesus Christ as Lord and Savior. We have given our lives, and continue to give our lives, to the mission of sharing the Good News: that God loves you, that He has a plan for your life, that you're trapped in sin and unable to connect with God, but He sent His Son Jesus to make the connection for you. You were doomed, but you can be saved. You can spend eternity in heaven with your loving heavenly Father. Accept Christ and live. Our family's message has never changed because God's offer has never changed, and no message has ever been more important to human beings.

For the sake of lost souls, over the course of my eighty-five years, I have traveled millions of miles. I have played and sung thousands of Gospel songs; I have lugged tons of equipment; I have pounded thousands of crusade tent stakes. I have preached thousands of sermons and given thousands more altar calls (for years I gave the altar calls at the end of my father's sermons).

For the sake of souls, I have raised and borrowed and spent about a billion dollars. I have built a church and left a church, both for the sake of souls.

For the sake of souls, I have gone hungry and I have eaten in the White House. I have challenged network television executives to their face. I have cried, and I have prayed.

For the sake of souls, I have dreamed up inventions to make evangelism more efficient. I have cooked up schemes to get around people who opposed evangelism. I have been reviled in the media and congratulated by world leaders.

For the sake of souls, I left my wife's bedside as she hovered near death.

For the sake of souls, I took money from Jimmy Hoffa.

For the sake of souls, I have prayed with Imelda Marcos and Elvis Presley and more than one dictator accused of war crimes.

For the sake of souls, I put my eldest son in seven different schools in a single year.

For the sake of souls, I left my father, my mother, and my brother.

For the sake of souls, I fought my way onto the radio, wheedled my way onto television, and finagled my way into building permits and on-air time slots and broadcast licenses.

For the sake of souls, I have built and operated a restaurant, yet over the course of my lifetime, I have fasted hundreds, maybe thousands of days.

For the sake of souls, I skipped college, and I bought a college.

For the sake of souls, I have sold girdles.

For the sake of souls, I have followed mysterious hunches and looked like a fool and kept trusting God.

For the sake of souls, I have preached to more than two hundred thousand people in a single gathering, and I have stopped to pray with a single troubled woman by the side of a road. I have been helped by kings and congressmen; I've been hassled by courts and cops. Other preachers have blessed me, betrayed me, berated me.

For the sake of souls, I've started building projects, stopped building projects, and torn up blueprints to start over in the middle of building projects. I've passed up lucrative business deals for the sake of souls. I've taken on questionable business partners for the sake of souls. I've dealt with mobsters, monks, Muslims, Methodists, and my wife, Maude Aimee—all for souls. I have been stolen from; I have been laughed at; I have been threatened; I have been cussed out—all for souls. I have hired people, fired people, refused handouts, taken handouts, pushed and pulled and zigzagged—all for souls. I have made brilliant decisions, and I have been a fool, but it was all for souls. Countless multitudes of people have received Christ as Savior as a result, and that's all I care about.

Here's the whole story of how it happened. My prayer is that, as you travel this road with me, you'll be drawn to trust Christ yourself and be inspired to give your own life to the cause of winning souls. If Jesus delays His return, the next century of soul winning is yours.

—REX HUMBARD

ONE

Odd to Be Called

*M*y father thought he was going to be murdered.

He was born Alpha Emmanuel Humbard in 1890 and was reared in a poor family on a farm in rural White County, Arkansas, some sixty miles north of Little Rock. His own father was a hard-scrabble farmer consumed by nothing but work. He had no education and didn't go to church. His parenting strategy was simple: keep the children busy.

My father's mother was a devoted Christian, but she died when he was two, after praying on her deathbed that her child would be called by God to preach the Gospel. My father didn't know this until years after he began preaching, when he heard the story from the woman who attended my grandmother at her death.

Something kept my father, in his youth, from joining the other boys in their Huck Finn mischief making: drinking, breaking glass out of vacant houses, stealing watermelons or chickens or eggs. His conscience repeatedly drove him away.

But it was odd that he would be called to preach. He had virtually no

5

education—three months a year in school more than two miles away, the rest doing chores on the farm—and often missed school because labor was too short in the fields to spare a child for a day in the classroom. He was also terribly bashful. And he had a speech impediment.

There were no family prayers. No Bible reading. No churchgoing. It was a stereotypical turn-of-the-century rural upbringing. The social scene outside Searcy, Arkansas, usually consisted of neighbors gathering in the evening to tell scary or off-color stories, play cards, drink liquor, hold the occasional dance, wind up in a fight, and knock out the lights. On top of it all, my grandfather had lost not only my grandmother but also a previous wife. He then married a third time, bringing additional children into the family, so he had four sets of children to deal with. My father's parents fought often, and loudly, with the children usually fleeing to safety under the house or into the barn.

Poverty was real. The children tasted candy only once a year, at Christmastime. Over the course of my father's entire childhood, there was only one exception: one year, his stepmother took the extraordinary measure of selling eggs to a chicken peddler for two cents per dozen and using the money to buy candy for her stepson's birthday.

A family of farmhands attended a church in town, and the children bragged about their Sunday school. Eventually my father sneaked away from Sunday chores and attended. Lured by an attendance promotion campaign—whoever attended the most Sundays would receive a small New Testament—my father continued slipping away on Sundays and heading to the church in town.

That little Testament changed my father's life. He carried it in his pocket everywhere he went, and with every available moment he read another portion of it. Plowing the fields, he had time at the end of each row as he let the mule rest to sit on the plow handles and read his Testament. He would meditate on the passage as he plowed the row, and then he'd begin the process again at the end of the line. He found himself believing the Word and asking God to help him live it. He also noticed that a lot of people in his world weren't living by the Bible!

ANGEL IN THE BEDROOM

Even in these early days of his life, my father experienced the power of practical faith. He wanted to give something in the Sunday school offering each week, but he never had anything of his own to give. So he asked God to help him find a penny sometime each week. Every week, without fail, he found a penny somewhere that he could place in the offering on Sunday.

His father kept liquor "as a medicine" and gave a small portion of it, a "toddy," to each child each morning before breakfast. When my father finally refused, he was whipped with a peach tree limb; but he continued refusing, and never touched alcohol again.

My father's family and friends couldn't understand his change. His friends started calling him "sissy." One day his father caught him praying behind a tree and told him he was losing his mind. Once a gang of boys caught him in the woods, held him down, and poured wine on his face and clothes. Another time, dressed up and on his way to church, they wallowed him in mud. But he was steadfast. He had connected with God, and God was real. He would not back down, look back, or change course.

> My father's family and friends couldn't understand his change. His friends started calling him "sissy."

My father claimed that an angel appeared in his bedroom one night and called his name three times. Sometime later, as he was plowing in the field, he heard God call his name "three times audibly, like He did

Samuel of old." It was my father's call to preach the Gospel, and it was like a "holy fire burning in his very bones." He argued with God about his lack of education, his speech impediment, and his bashfulness. But as he was reminded of Moses overcoming very similar difficulties in Exodus 4, he didn't have much leverage to resist God's call.

He decided that too many people were dying and going to hell each day for him to spend time wading through seminary. He did not sense a call to seminary; he sensed a call to evangelism. My father, according to what would become a lifelong pattern, took the simplest and straightest route to the goal.

He had what he regarded as a good job with a banker who liked him, with the promise of ready promotions. Continuing to work at the bank by day, he attached himself to a preacher who was holding evening revival services in a nearby country schoolhouse. The preacher had asked my father to sit next to him on the platform, which mortified the young man. Eventually he got over his stage fright, although the first time he was called upon to give his testimony, his knees knocked together so badly that he fell back in his chair.

Soon he knew the time had come when he would have to leave his banking job and pursue his ministry full time. His only puzzle was the question of which church he should represent. There were three Christian churches in town, each claiming to be the "one true church"; and a man from Kansas passing through town had said that there were 650 denominations total. My father was so perplexed by the question that early one Sunday morning he climbed to the top of a mountain with his Bible, prayed and fasted all day, asking God for an answer. As night began to fall, he still had no direction. But as he prepared to head home, he sensed God speaking to his spirit, telling him to let his Bible fall open; the answer would appear. My father did so, and his Bible opened to John 14:6: "I am the way, the truth, and the life."

"The Baptist was not crucified for you," the Spirit of God said to my father in that moment. "The Methodist was not buried or resurrected the third day for your justification. I am *the* Way (not *a* way), the Truth, the Life. I am the Door. I am the Bread. I am the Living Water. There is no other Name under heaven whereby man can be saved, only by Me."

From that moment, Alpha Humbard worked with any church or group that claimed Christ and followed the Bible. "There are only two families in the world," he said: "God's family and the devil's family. By one Spirit we are all baptized into the one body of which the Lord Jesus is the Head." Beyond that, Dad didn't do doctrine.

"I Feel You're Called"

Knowing almost nothing about the kind of life and work to which he felt called, my father began asking God to send a preacher to help him get started in his ministry. Inside of a week, a preacher arrived from 400 miles away with no invitation, just a sense that God had led him to this out-of-the-way community. The preacher, Alonzo Horn, began holding revival meetings in a schoolhouse five miles below my father's town. My father walked from the bank to the schoolhouse every night to see Horn preach a "hellfire and brimstone" Gospel. For three weeks, not a single person responded to the altar calls or even raised a hand for prayer, but Horn was undaunted. He preached the Word night after night. Suddenly one evening, for no apparent reason, the people began to weep as the man closed his sermon. More than a third of the people ran for the altar. Some knelt in the aisles. Three men fell to the floor like dead men, only to revive with noisy praises to God. My father had never seen anything like it.

That evening, Horn came to my father. "I feel like you're called to preach," he said. It was a stunning confirmation; my father had never mentioned his calling.

The two agreed to travel together in ministry. When the local revival ended, my father rolled up a spare shirt in a piece of paper, and put on his one good suit of clothes, which he had long ago outgrown. The trousers only reached the middle of his calves; the sleeves were halfway to his elbows. But he was on his way to a lifetime in evangelistic ministry.

The day he left home, he had never before ridden on a train. He had never seen an automobile. He had never owned a necktie. Their first stop was Little Rock, a gargantuan metropolis, from his view. A streetcar looked to him like a wagon shed being dragged by horses, but without horses.

For months he simply served as the older preacher's assistant, shining his shoes and sweeping out the meeting places and carrying water and praying for him as the old man preached. After about six months, in Huntington, Arkansas, Horn sent him out to conduct street meetings each evening before the services. The strategy worked; crowds overflowed the one-thousand-seat meeting place, forcing them to move to a sprawling open area and add services. At a special Sunday afternoon service with nearly four thousand attending, Horn turned to my father during the musical worship and informed him that he would be delivering the sermon. My father sputtered his objections, but Horn had decided. "You might just as well start now as some other time," he said.

My father stood terrified before the huge crowd. He opened his Bible, read a text, and suddenly felt the Spirit of God burning within him. Then, as he opened his mouth, he found that he was speaking French. He had never studied or even heard the language. Eventually he switched to English, and found that the Scriptures were coming to his mind faster than he could quote them. His years of studying God's Word at the plow handle were now bearing fruit.

As he finished his sermon, more than three thousand people were weeping. It turned out that there was a large French-speaking community in Huntington, with scores of French-speaking people in attendance at the meeting. They rushed forward as the service ended.

"This man can't speak good English," one laughed, "but he spoke the French language very plainly!"

They quizzed my father about his background, certain that he must be of French origin. But he was dumbfounded—simply a vessel to be used by the Spirit of God—and many of the French people of the community came to Christ that day!

My father's mentor, Alonzo Horn, was astonished. "I don't think I will try to preach anymore around you," he said wryly. "You got me skinned. I never saw anything like it."

So my father headed out into ministry alone.

MOONSHINE AND MINISTRY

Evangelism, difficult enough in my day and difficult in different ways today, could be brutal in the early 1900s. To preach Christ in middle America in my father's day was in many ways as dangerous as missionary work among hostile tribes. In many of the rough, wide-open back-country towns of the pre-World War I era, local leaders—judges, bankers, merchants, even some clergymen—were financially involved in saloons, gambling houses, and other shady enterprises. So the arrival of a Bible preacher crusading against sin and moral corruption was not greeted with warm enthusiasm.

Accordingly, the day came when my father found himself in what he later described as "a very rough community" in rural Arkansas. The common term for the people of such an area in those days was "hillbilly," but that doesn't seem to communicate their response to my dad's ministry. Many of the locals wore red handkerchiefs around their necks and carried a gun or a pair of brass knuckles.

Nevertheless, my father began an evangelistic crusade in a "hillbilly" community. Scores of people came to Christ, but this was regarded as bad news by the rougher elements in town. Among the most disturbed was a local preacher whom my father considered crooked. His cronies included people who claimed to be Christian but were active makers and sellers of moonshine. They formed a mob, went to the local Masonic Temple where my father's meetings were being held, and waited secretly behind the building until the service was over and the crowd had departed.

As my father and his companion, the singer and worship leader, turned out the last of the lights, the mob pounced. They carried the pair toward the jailhouse.

"Where's the key?" one of them asked.

"We're not going to put them in jail," the ringleader growled. "We have other plans."

They marched their prisoners down a road that ended up running along a river.

My father offered no resistance; he could imagine his captors tying a weight around his neck and throwing him in the river, but he was praying silently and trusting the Lord. Near the end of the road was a large tree.

"Here's the place!" one of the men cried.

My father thought he and the singer were about to be hanged.

"Carry them on," one of the men ordered instead, "over on the railroad."

Now my dad was sure of the plan: the men would tie him to a rail—the "fast train" was due in about twenty minutes—letting the enormous machinery crush him to death.

Like so many who have faced imminent death, my father saw his life flash before his eyes. He thought of ways he could have been wiser, accomplished more, acted more kindly. He imagined how his family would mourn.

But he was ready to go. He was firmly "reconciled to the Lord," as he put it. He paraphrased Romans 8:18 to himself: "These little light afflictions of suffering will not be worthy to be compared with the glory that He reveals in us over there." He thought of the morning papers carrying the story of his murder.

"My folks and friends will be made sad," he thought, "but I'll be up in heaven, walking the golden streets, and taking dinner with Jesus!"

But suddenly the leader of the mob gave new orders: "Take him through that wire fence, out where the rest of the bunch is."

Beside a small lake were gasoline torches hanging on trees, small tables and kegs of beer. A number of revelers were drinking, gambling, and "carrying on."

"Well, here they are, boys," the mob leader announced. "Cut you a big hickory switch. We're going to give them a whipping."

My father almost laughed with joy, discovering that he was going to be whipped instead of killed!

Someone cut a switch about six feet long, leaving the small limbs and sharp snouts in place. One man, half drunk, made my father remove his coat and clothing; then he pulled my dad's shirt up around his neck. Another man took him by the hair, cursing him and pulling him forward until his chin touched his knees. The man propped my father against his knees to hold him steady and to keep the skin on his back as tight as possible.

The man with the whip took the weapon in both his hands. Each lick cut a gash from four to six inches long on the stretched flesh. The pain was severe at first, but my father sensed God speaking to him: "You remember in my Word that I promise: if you can believe, all things are possible. So believe it won't hurt anymore."

My father—simple of faith, full of trust—did as he had been told. The rest of the lashes, he recounted later, felt like nothing more than children "hitting me with some strings."

13

"Get out of town tonight," the assailants said when they were finished, "or we'll kill you."

As my father staggered away, he found that blood was sloshing in his shoes as if he had gone wading. On his back was a ghastly square that looked, in my father's words, as if someone "had taken a hammer and beat up a beefsteak to fry."

He and his friend followed the railroad tracks to the edge of town. There, as they sat by the tracks, my father sensed an angel of God standing next to him, speaking comfort to him.

It was an opportunity for hate, for resentment and revenge. But instead, my father found to his own surprise that a great love bubbled up in his spirit. "I loved them and pitied them," he said. "I knew that they were some mothers' darling children, and that they had souls, and Jesus had died for them."

While the men were still sitting there, word of the assault was spreading through town. One man grabbed his gun. He wasn't a Christian, but he had attended the revival meetings and was seeking God. He formed a gang of men "to protect that preacher." They searched for the pair in vain for an hour, and were finally heading home in despair when they were stopped by a strange being who asked if they were looking for "the preacher." By his description, it was the same angel that had visited my father. "You will find him on the railroad tracks," the being told the group, "sitting by the road." Then he vanished. The men, frightened, ran to find my father, exactly where the angel had directed them. (The leader of the group, along with his daughter, a notorious sinner, later came to faith in Christ through the experience!)

The group gave assistance to my father and his friend, and the next day the two of them breezed back into town, walking up and down the streets looking for members of the mob. They wanted to assure them of their love and forgiveness—and God's. But those who saw them coming turned and fled. One panicked and broke down the screen door of a café to escape. A lawyer from the county seat arrived on the scene before day's end and offered to sue at the state level. He would advance my father ten thousand dollars against the judgment he knew the court would make.

But my father declined.

"Vengeance is mine; I will repay, saith the Lord," Romans 12:19 reminded him. If Jesus had gone to the law every time someone said or did anything to Him, my father reasoned, He would have been in a lawsuit all the time. He never would have had time to go about His Father's business.

"I'm going to turn this case over to the Lord," my dad told the lawyer, "and lay this ten thousand dollars up in heaven for future rewards. I will turn these men over to the Lord to deal with them as He sees fit."

The lawyer was furious. "You're a fool!" he declared. "If I had been there, I would have helped them to whip you!"

My father proceeded to pray for the salvation of the members of the mob, but their demise was ugly. Within ninety days, four of the men had died: one from a sudden massive stroke, one from a mental breakdown, a third—a doctor who brazenly declared that he was not afraid of God and the world would be better off if all the preachers were killed and the churches burned—simply slumped over dead at the dinner table. The man who had whipped my father, a railroad worker, died a horrible death in a freak accident, his head crushed between two boxcars.

The fifth man in the mob, a judge, lived, but he testified a quarter century later that he had "never seen a moment's peace" from the day he participated in the whipping of the preacher. He and his wife had both suffered poor health; they had struggled with their children. His life was hell on earth.

Some thirty years later, Dad heard a radio report of a tornado destroying the community where he had been whipped. "I've got to go back up

15

there and see what happened to that judge," he said. Our family at the time was ministering in Houston, Texas, but my father got in his car, in spite of World War II gas rationing, and drove to Arkansas. The destruction was horrible, and police had cordoned off the area; they let Dad pass because he was a clergyman. The tornado had completely wrecked the judge's home; the judge had been killed. Strangely, the tornado's twisting tower of gales had been moving in a straight line across the countryside, following the path of a highway that ran from north to south about two miles from the center of town. But as the tornado drew near the town, it made a sudden sharp detour, circled around to the east, smashed the center of town, killed the judge, demolished his house, and then returned to its original path beside the highway!

It was typical of my dad that he rarely told this story of persecution. In fact, he had been in ministry nearly forty years before he wrote a book about his life and experiences. Even then, he related the story of his capture and whipping as more or less just another bump on the Gospel road.

ON THE "FAITH LINE"

When my father headed home to Searcy, Arkansas, where the locals told him he couldn't get a crowd, he found they were right. On the first night of his revival, he stood before an empty hall, gave a welcome, sang a couple songs, prayed, read his Scripture text, and preached for thirty minutes.

"I closed my eyes," he recalled years later, "and by faith I could see every seat full."

At the end of his sermon, he made an announcement to the still-empty room: "There will be services here tomorrow night. Come early or you will miss something. We are going to begin on time."

At home his stepmother asked if anyone had come out for his meeting. Yes, my father replied: "Me, the Lord, and the devil."

By day he went into the woods, praying as much as eight hours per day. By night he returned to the empty building and held services all alone. On the third night a local merchant heading home after a day's work happened to look in the window. My father didn't see him, but the merchant was transfixed by the man and his message. He ran from business to business telling people about the local boy who was preaching "like the world was on fire." The businessman even broke up a city council meeting to spread the news.

The next night, my father preached to a nearly full house, and the following evening the building was packed, with people standing outside around the windows. Business people, lawyers, doctors, and bankers were among them. People were astonished to see "little Alpha," whom they remembered as a skinny, bashful, tongue-tied, seventh-grade dropout who couldn't even give a speech in school, now speaking with such boldness. Revival broke out through my father's hometown meetings. He took scores of converts down to the river and baptized them.

> **Revival broke out through my father's hometown meetings. He took scores of converts down to the river and baptized them.**

Led only by the Spirit of God, my father moved all over the middle of the country, mostly Arkansas and Oklahoma, holding revival meetings. Wherever he was given the opportunity, my father would preach. He was so on fire for God that he had a hard time ending a sermon. Talking to other ministers, he got particularly wound up. At one preachers' convention, he spoke for three hours and forty-five minutes; at another, six hours without stopping for a drink of water. At one meeting in Oklahoma he preached till midnight, stopped to serve communion, then preached again till daylight.

He was single-minded. He spent his time reading the Bible, meditating on the Scriptures, praying, and fasting. He stayed in people's homes, sometimes in wretched rooms, in barns and sheds and train depots, on benches. He learned the power of prayer, the reality of faith. He preached in churches, in schools, in outdoor brush arbors. He ministered among the poorest of the poor, staying in homes where the children had head lice, where flies or mosquitoes swarmed in the house, where the mattress was full of bedbugs, where the food had worms in it, or where—most disgusting of all to my father—they dipped snuff, chewed tobacco, and spat.

He lived his life on what he called "the faith line." In the first eight years, he took no collections in his meetings; he lived exclusively by prayer and faith, trusting God to meet every need. He preached the Gospel, and thousands of people received Christ. He stayed in a place until he sensed the Lord leading him to move on. In many cases he bought a train ticket only as far as the money in his pocket could carry him. He would go into the station and ask God to lead him. Sometimes he would strike up a conversation. Somehow God always provided, even though my father never talked about his financial need, often by people feeling inexplicably prompted to give him lodging, meals, money, or some other help.

When he heard about a huge "worldwide religious convention" in California, he felt God leading him to attend. The cost would be enormous, yet he never mentioned his desire to go, and God supernaturally provided the funds for a train ticket. My father had never been to California before; had never seen the ocean, never eaten in a cafeteria, never even seen linoleum.

His clothes grew threadbare over time, and a kind preacher gave him a scissor-bill coat. It embarrassed my father greatly, but he had no other coat to wear. For weeks he prayed that God would somehow provide him a different coat, but nothing happened. Only when my father finally felt convicted about his pride, caring so much about what people thought of his appearance, did a group of preachers take pity on him and buy him a normal-looking suit of clothes.

Christians in one Missouri community had purchased a tent, and they invited my father to preach the inaugural revival campaign. The meetings were a tremendous success; many were saved and baptized, their lives profoundly changed by the power of God's love. A man stood up in one meeting and introduced himself as a merchant from a town five miles away. "This meeting has stirred this whole country," he declared. "I have collected thirty-two hundred dollars on old store accounts that were ten and fifteen years old. I had thrown the books back in the safe and never expected to get the old accounts paid. People must be getting religion! They pay up their old debts and make restitution and ask each other's forgiveness."

As the Missouri revival drew to a close, my father planned to head back to his hometown, but his family wrote to say there was no facility available for such big meetings. Not knowing how God would move, my father continued preparing to leave Missouri for Arkansas.

Before he left town, two men came to him and informed him that they wanted to give him a gift before his departure. He had never taken an offering in the entire revival campaign, but now they handed him a sizable donation. They weren't finished, however; there was something else. They were giving him the tent.

Dad joyfully shipped the tent home to Searcy, Arkansas.

This was the first of many Humbard tents. It was also the first of many facilities-related challenges and conflicts, because when he got home, Dad found that the local authorities would not let him put up his tent on any public land. But as usual, my father simply prayed and trusted God, and God worked in the strangest of ways.

There was a hard-bitten "infidel" living in town, a man who owned forty acres. One corner of the land came to a point just two blocks from the bank and the post office. The man had run into conflicts with the city fathers; they had refused a license he needed and had effectively run him out of business. So he had a grudge against the city leaders.

When he heard my father needed a place to put up his tent, he told him to put it up on his land, as close to downtown as possible, at the end of one of the main streets. "Just cut my wire fence and set the tent on the inside," he said. "Leave a gap open for people to come from the end of the street into the tent."

What if someone objected?

"If necessary, I will sit out there with my shotgun and protect the place," the man growled. "Nobody in this town better do you any harm, or harm this tent which is setting on my land!"

People came as far as fifty miles to attend the revival. My father baptized 120 people, most of them his own aunts, uncles, cousins, and one of his half-brothers who had bitterly persecuted him in their childhood.

The hometown revival rolled on and on. "You could go all over town," Dad said, "in the barber shop and the business houses and even at night in the alleys and streets, and all around the railroad station" and hear people talking about God, talking about the revival, and singing Christian songs. Traveling salesmen tried to get back home on the weekends so they wouldn't miss meetings. The movie theater had to close for lack of attendance. The local Methodist minister threatened to do my father bodily harm, but the criticism just increased attendance in the revival meetings!

TIME FOR A TABERNACLE

Eventually Dad felt led by God to build a large tabernacle in town, "a union church where Christians of all denominations could worship together." It had been a hard year; the crops had burned up. His cousin's husband, a contractor, scoffed at the idea. "You couldn't raise enough out of this bunch of poor people to build a chicken coop!" he sneered.

But my father felt he had heard from God, so he sat down and proceeded to design a tabernacle, a building unlike any he had ever observed or heard about. He also prepared a pledge form, wrote his own name at the top, and promised by faith to give twenty-five dollars cash along with his own labor.

People laughed. They knew he didn't have a dollar to his name.

"And we don't have the money to give you," someone said.

"Well, I'm not trusting you," Dad replied. "I'm trusting the Lord, and the Lord will send it in by the time we need it."

No one would pledge, however, and no one would give. After several days of this paralysis, my father began fasting and praying, asking God to remove the people's doubt.

One morning the contractor said to his wife, my father's cousin, "I feel sorry for Alpha." But he didn't want to help him; he just wanted to get this silly tabernacle idea out of his head and put him out of his misery. He decided to take the pledge form around to several local businessmen and get firsthand rejections. "That will show him he can't get anything," he told his wife. "It will satisfy him, and he'll quit talking about faith all the time and what can be done."

First he visited the head of a sawmill who had been powerfully touched by God in my father's first hometown meetings. He looked at the pledge form and listened to the idea for a new tabernacle. But instead of sending the contractor away, he pointed to a pile of shingles. "If that preacher wanted to build a tabernacle that would cover two acres of land," he said, "I'll furnish all the shingles needed, free of charge. I'll even haul them around to the spot!"

The surprised contractor moved on to a lumber company. The owner was an alcoholic; but his wife had been converted to Christ and healed in

21

my father's first meeting in town. "My home has been changed," the man told the contractor. "For twenty years I spent nearly everything I could get for medicine and doctors, to no avail. Now she is perfectly well and doing all the housework. It has not cost me one penny in medicine and doctors since she has been converted, and she has gained at least twenty pounds."

And he refused to have his business outdone by the sawmill. "We'll give as much lumber as the amount of shingles he's giving," the man promised.

A third company owner promised to match the others, delivering lumber to the site every evening: studding, ceiling, and rafters. Other businesspeople promised cash. By noon the contractor came running through his own front door, all out of breath with the good news.

"This is the way most people are," my father observed years later as he recounted this story. "They think they've got faith, after they see a lot of things done, but faith in reality is to believe a thing when it's dark as midnight and not a straw to hang your hopes on. Faith will reach out and say, 'It can be done.'"

The ball began rolling. People wanted to give money or labor or both. By faith, Dad paid a little down on a lot and began building. The tabernacle went up: thirty by sixty feet, with the side walls hinged so that they looked like regular walls but could be swung open in the summer, allowing cool air in and offering extra space for seats. Dad began meetings in the building before the ceiling was in. He did most of the ceiling work himself, sometimes preaching in his overalls for lack of time to change. He often began work again after services, sometimes working till three in the morning, until the building was finished. The newspaper ran a big story on the tabernacle as one of the finest and best-built churches in the county.

It was also a breakthrough for evangelism. No one had ever heard of holding revival meetings in the wintertime, because they were typically held in tents and it was too cold to meet in a tent in winter weather. Now my father could stage evangelistic events year round. His passion for reaching lost souls could burn continuously.

My father did pay his twenty-five dollar pledge, by the way. Every few days his cousin, the contractor's wife, would quiz him about it. "Where are you going to get this twenty-five dollars? I can't keep from worrying about it." My father's response was straightforward: "Worrying is not faith. You cannot worry and have faith at the same time, as one of them has to cease in order for the other to work." Just days before the pledge was due, he found a letter in his mailbox from an acquaintance with whom he had never corresponded—ironically from the California town of Eureka. "The Lord spoke to me," the letter said, "saying, 'Send Brother Humbard $25 at once,' so I am obeying the Lord by mailing it to you." My father, faith filled as he was, more or less shrugged. "Of course, this was no surprise to me," he said with a smile. But the news of this surprise gift inspired the faith of scores of people, who then experienced the joy of God's blessing as they gave freely toward the tabernacle and trusted Him to meet their needs.

> **"Worrying is not faith. You cannot worry and have faith at the same time, as one of them has to cease in order for the other to work."**

Today, decades later, I see in my father's experience the foreshadowing of my own ministry: the tent, followed by the dream of a permanent church with an unprecedented design—accompanied by doubt and faith, discouragement and generosity, sweat and blessing—and the astonished acclaim of the world. Even before I was born—in fact, before my father had even met my mother—my destiny was being shaped. The shape of modern evangelism was being established. Our Cathedral of

Tomorrow and our worldwide television ministry were unimaginable back then, before the Roaring Twenties had even arrived, but the fire in my father's heart was setting the stage.

And I would, soon enough, download his evangelist's chromosomes.

INSTEAD OF REVENGE

My father had one other unique quality: he had no capacity for revenge.

As he pastored the tabernacle over a number of years, he also occasionally "jumped out," in his words, to hold revivals in other communities. During one such absence, one preacher who substituted for him at the tabernacle turned out to have an ulterior motive. He "tried to tear up my church, or divide them," Dad recalled, "but he was not successful in this." Upon my father's return to town, the preacher decided to stage another revival nearby.

Dad went to them and tried to talk about it, but they were unreasonable. They had plans to bring in a hot-shot preacher from Louisiana. The preacher who had begun it all had the audacity to write to my father and ask, pretending innocence, where he could buy a tent. Dad knew what he wanted a tent for. But he also knew what he had long ago memorized from Romans 12:21: "Do not be overcome by evil, but overcome evil with good."

So my father sold him his tent!

I am astonished to review the historical records and see what happened next. The group actually erected the tent in a grove almost next door to Dad's tabernacle. The preacher ostensibly preached from the Bible, but almost every night his sermon was about my father. Sometimes he did impersonations of my father and called him names.

The fellow drew great crowds at first; it was cool under the tent. Soon the preacher announced that they needed more chairs.

Then one day my father happened to meet him on the street.

"Why, good morning, brother!" my father crowed. "How are you?" And he shook hands with the man. "How are your meetings coming along? I hear that you need some more seats. I'll tell you what I'll do. We have no special revival on now, so you can have half of my seats or more. And if you're short of money, I'll pay the transfer man to move them."

The next day, my father made good on his promise and sent the chairs over.

A couple days later the preacher announced to his crowd that they needed an organ. Dad had a new one in the tabernacle. When he ran into the man at the post office, he told him he'd send a man over with the organ right away.

That night the preacher announced he needed someone to play the organ. The next day my father was in his face: "I'll let my wife come over and play it for you," he said happily.

"Give the devil the biggest end of the rope," my father often told me, "and he'll hang himself."

My father proceeded to tell the people of his own church to attend the man's services. Dad even attended himself. "Several people believed and were converted," my father recalled with satisfaction. One young man was converted as my mother sang "Sin Is to Blame." He went on to become a preacher of the Gospel himself!

But soon the spoiler's revival blew over. All the people who came to Christ in those meetings wound up attending my father's church. His ministry grew larger than ever. Within a year or so, the opposition movement had faded. Strangely, the two main leaders of the effort were smitten by a dreadful disease and soon died.

More than once my father related an old saying that began, "Nearly everybody picks on the preacher." It went, in part:

If he dresses up, he's a snob; if he goes common, he's a bum....

If he gets up a good sermon, he's too smart for his own good; if he don't get up any, he's lazy.

If he takes offerings, then he's preaching for money; if he don't take any, he will starve. If he has legal, law-abiding credentials, then he has the mark of the beast; if he has none, he isn't right....

If he exposes sin, he has the wrong spirit; if he covers up sin, he's a hypocrite.

When the opposition revival faded, my father was as philosophical as ever about it.

"Sometimes it is better to lose for the time being and show the Christlike spirit, and gain in the long run," he said. "It is best always to let the Lord fight our battles, as He always wins."

I would need that advice in the decades ahead.

THE SPIRIT SPEAKS GERMAN

My father could not leave well enough alone. He was constantly pleading with God for lost souls, incessantly asking for opportunities to reach more people with the Gospel. Again and again, people asked him to leave the tabernacle and come to their own communities to hold evangelistic meetings.

In one meeting, a man jumped up and interrupted the sermon.

"Preacher, are you German?" he cried.

My father replied that he was not.

"Do you speak the German language?" the man asked.

My father, having no idea why the man was asking, admitted that he did not.

"I know you do," the man insisted, "and I cannot understand how you found out so many things about me. A few minutes ago you were speaking the German language very plainly and looked right at me and told me my name, how old I was, and all the devilment and meanness that I ever did, and that if I didn't repent of it I was going to be lost."

My father was stunned. This was all news to him! He had simply been preaching a sermon under the guidance of the Holy Spirit!

"I thank God that my wife and my children were not here today," the man continued, "because if she heard the things you told me, she would leave me; and my children would have nothing to do with me!"

He walked down the aisle, fell on his face before God, and wept. "I heard you speak the wonderful Word of God in my own language," he insisted. And he was gloriously converted. That same evening he brought his wife and eight children back to the church, where they all heard the Gospel and came to Christ.

The revival eventually closed, and a local preacher complained to my father when he happened to run into him, "I don't understand how you had such a revival at this place," he said. "I don't think it's fair! I went to college and prepared myself and can talk good English. Then I went down there for meetings and only two or three would come out, and we also had a conference for three days and there were six of us preachers, and only from two or three to a dozen people came out. Sometimes there were more preachers than there were people. It is one of the hardest places I ever saw! Then you go down there and have a big revival.... I think the people are not treating me fair. Here I am, a learned man and speak good English and spent my money to go to school, and you—an old farm boy, a clodhopper who can't talk good English—then the people rally around you and have a big revival. It makes me mad!"

My father recounted the conversation with a smile, adding at the end: "While he was talking, he was smoking a cigar." My father recommended that he throw away the cigar and get on his knees and "pray a little bit."

Truly, my father was not impressed by the supernatural ways in which God chose to work through him. "When His Spirit gets in you and has His way," he said, "many miraculous things will happen. Well, why not? When that Spirit begins to move upon you, that Spirit through whom the Lord made the heaven and earth, moon, sun and stars, and delivered Daniel from the lions' den, the Hebrew children from the fiery furnace, made an ax to swim, created water in the jawbone of a dead beast for Samson to get a drink, increased oil in the widow's can, turned water to wine at the marriage feast of Cana, caused money to be created in the mouth of a fish for Peter to catch and pay their taxes with, and caused three thousand Jews to be converted on the Day of Pentecost, turned a whole city of Samaria from sorcery and spiritualism to serve the Living God—if that Spirit is in you, and you yield to the Lord and let Him work, anything can happen!"

My father was not afraid to pray for people to be healed. He took God at His word and believed that the Lord could just as easily heal sick people today as He did in the days of Jesus's earthly ministry. In a California meeting, a distraught mother asked him to pray for her daughter, who wore a huge platform under one shoe because her legs were six inches different in length. My father was not given to long, loud, emotional prayers; he prayed just a few words. When he was finished, the girl tried to walk away, but she was now limping badly. Dad told her to sit down. He pulled off her orthopedic shoe. She was limping because her legs were now the same length!

He saw smallpox healed in two minutes. A grotesque facial cancer became perfectly smooth. A woman with acute appendicitis and unable to get medical help was close to death until my father prayed for her; she immediately sat up, completely healthy. It was all "normal" to Dad, because he trusted God to work! He saw blind eyes opened, deaf ears unstopped, tuberculosis cured—all through prayer.

Sometimes God would give him advance notice of future events, or insights into the hidden details of a person's situation. This "gift of prophecy" didn't trouble my father, but it generally got the attention of the people he prophesied about! One evening in a church service, God gave him a vision of a local man's "danger and death"; my father went to the man and tried to persuade him to turn to God before he left the building. The man was offended. He was in good health; he had never been sick a day in his life, and he was "not going to be scared by a preacher." He went home. That night his breathing became congested and he had chills. In three days he was dead. My father preached his funeral.

To look back on my father's life and ministry now, one might categorize him as a "holiness" preacher. He often said, "I don't care how high you jump in my meetings, if you will walk straight when you hit the ground." But my father was very practical about "holiness." He didn't see a lot of advantage in pressuring people to act in a certain supposed holy way. His rationale was typically homespun, but surprisingly sophisticated.

"The reason people have measles," he explained, "is that they get the germ in their blood and then the bumps pop out. You don't have to try to have measles; they will have you. Neither do you have to force yourself to live like a Christian. If we will believe the Gospel and read the Word of God, we will get the germ in our spirit stream. Then the good works and right living will automatically pop out on us, and we won't have to try to be a Christian; we will just be one because we are one. It's Christ in you, the hope of glory."

On a Street Called Cross

My father first laid eyes on my mother at a convention in Eureka Springs, Arkansas. He had determined to "live like the apostle Paul," never marrying. But he fell hard the moment he saw her, and he always claimed that God told him in that moment that he would have her someday as his wife.

In the careful society of the day, he couldn't simply strike up a conversation with her. His love tortured him throughout the meetings, and when he left town he still didn't even know her name. But he trusted God to have told him the truth; she would be his.

At a state camp meeting a full year later, he saw her again, and this time he mustered the courage to find out her name "in a roundabout way." She was Martha Bell Childers, the daughter of a preacher and already active in ministry herself for years. She was traveling as an assistant to Mother Barnes, a famous evangelist of the day who had led Martha to Christ, and he learned later that she had fallen for him at first sight too. He began walking her home from services. On the second walk, he asked her to marry him. They were married a year later at Heber Springs, Arkansas, and settled in Pangburn, where my father was based as pastor of a tabernacle.

Within days she was struck down in the massive influenza epidemic that took so many lives at the end of World War I. Almost too weak to walk, she insisted on going to church and singing in the choir. In the middle of the service, she was suddenly and miraculously healed.

It was the beginning of a lifetime of walking by faith together. My parents preached, sang, held evangelistic meetings, and pastored churches faithfully year after year. They routinely did as much as they could and then some more. As my father was still pastoring the tabernacle in his hometown, he appointed an assistant to lead the charge in his absence while he and my mother took a pastorate in Little Rock. There, on a street called Cross on the thirteenth of August, I was born, Alpha Rex Emmanuel Humbard.

TWO

Training Up

The first words I can recall hearing were the prayers of my parents.

Having traveled a lot in ministry, staying in many families' homes, both of my parents had seen their share of unruly children. They determined that they would spoil their children too, but in a different way. "We spoiled them to lie on the bed and to be quiet," my father always said. "Some people say it is so much trouble to raise children right, but I find that it is a greater trouble to worry with them later on because you did not raise them right."

They took me to church, laid me on a pallet behind the piano, and told me to go to sleep. My instructions were to lie still until after the service. By the third service, and the third spanking, I played my part perfectly. When they traveled to minister in evangelistic meetings in other towns, their hosts often failed to realize that they even had a child!

One week when Dad was preaching at a Gospel meeting in Webb City, Missouri, we stayed with a young couple who had a little girl about my age, less than two years old. The little girl teased me mercilessly.

During the nightly services, when I was tucked into my pallet behind the piano, her parents allowed her to run loose all over the church. One evening during the opening preliminaries, the little girl came over to me, punched me, then ran off, taunting me to chase her. I got up on one elbow (so my father said when he related the story), looked at her, looked at Dad, and lay back down. But just before he began to preach, he heard four little feet crossing the stage. I could stand it no longer and had taken off after her. My father picked me up, laid me across the lectern, and gave me a good spanking. When he set me down, he didn't have to tell me where to go. I beat it back to the pallet, stuck my finger in my mouth, and went to sleep. Dad proceeded to throw out the sermon he had planned and instead preached on raising children right: "Train up a child in the way he should go; and when he is old, he will not depart from it," quoting from Proverbs 22:6.

I grew up, literally, in ministry and never knew another way. My parents established a daily "family altar," and we came together in prayer and Bible reading every day without fail. We often had to live near "gambling houses, ill-famed places, and saloons," as my father described them, but my parents never had any trouble with me, nor with my brother and sisters who came along after me. Ministry was our life. Evangelism was our mission. Christ was our Leader.

> **Ministry was our life. Evangelism was our mission. Christ was our Leader.**

My sister Ruth was born a year and a half after me; then came my brother, Clement, and three more sisters: Leona, Mary, and Juanita. The offerings from Dad's congregations in the grim Depression years did not amount to much. When there was no food in the house, Mom would say, "Get out the pots and pans and put them on the stove, and we'll pray to God to fill them. He's never let us down yet." And He never did.

32

A Quarter of an Apple

My parents were heartbroken to see children suffering, and while we lived and ministered for a time in Pangburn, Arkansas, we established an orphanage which eventually held sixty children. In the natural, it was crazy. There wasn't much to eat, and money was terribly tight. At one point a rural mother left her four children on the bank of a river downstream from Pangburn; it was raining, and I imagine she hoped they would slide into the river and drown, because she couldn't bring herself to push them in. But they wound up with us. At Christmastime, there was no money for gifts, or even a special meal; the only novelty was a few apples and oranges. My mother halved them, in hopes of giving some to each child, but she was still going to turn up short, so she quartered the fruit. And ultimately, she still didn't have enough for all the children.

I was sitting on a little step that led down into the room where all the orphans were getting their piece of fruit. I could see that I wasn't going to get any myself, and my mother saw me sitting there; she knew I was disappointed. She gave all the precious fruit away, and then stepped over to me.

"Rex, you don't understand now," she said quietly, "but someday you will." She couldn't explain it. She could only do what she knew she had to do. It pained her to take a quarter of an apple from her own son, but she did it to give to someone in need.

Years later, I understood what she was saying. I would come to value my faith so deeply that I would give up everything, whatever it took, to share it with people in need.

The Great Pit of Fire

At eight years of age, I was picking cotton to help my family make ends meet. In the heat of a summer day, I suffered what looked like sun stroke. My mother certainly didn't know what to do with me—this was the

1920s—so she got cold rags and put them on my head all night long. The next day I regained consciousness. My mother had a question for me: "Rex, why were you swinging your arms and fighting the air, yelling and screaming all night long?"

I had an answer: "Mom, there was a great big pit of fire," I told her, "and the flames were coming up out of it. All around it were thousands and thousands of people, and there were men on horses like soldiers, with spears, and they were pushing these people off into the fire. I was there, trying to keep them from pushing those people into the fire."

It had been a long night for an eight-year-old boy, but I sensed, even then, that God put something in my heart. I would never get away from that vision of hell. It would become a driving force for me, trying to keep people from falling into the fire, from going to hell. To this day, I never have been able to lead a church service without giving an invitation for people to make the decision to stay out of that pit, to stay out of that fire. As a result, mine has been a message of salvation. I believe in healing; I believe in miracles. But I felt called from the beginning to reach people with the message of salvation, inviting people to dedicate their lives to the Lord Jesus Christ.

"No" Means Nothing

Year by year, as I grew up, our family moved around in ministry. We generally didn't know where we were going to be sleeping, what we were going to be eating, or how any of these details were going to be arranged, except by the divine intervention of God our Father. We ministered throughout the Great Depression, sometimes taking food instead of pay. Our clothes became threadbare; we had holes in the soles of our shoes. My father cut a piece of cardboard and put it in the bottom of his shoes to keep his feet off the ground. Then when holes poked through the toes of his shoes, he began putting shoe polish on his socks so his problem wouldn't be so noticeable.

Hot Springs, however, was more or less our home base. My father held a revival there and then felt led by God to look for a large building to rent as a church. He found a filthy vacant theater—vacant except for forty hoboes who spent nights there—its windows nailed over with lumber. It had a large auditorium with the equivalent of an eighteen-room apartment upstairs. The Spirit of God fell upon my dad when he walked in: "This is the place; go rent it."

He learned that a banker owned the building. The banker turned my father down flat. It wasn't for rent. He wouldn't rent it "for love or money at any price." Besides, the banker pointed out, "It's in bad condition." What an understatement!

But as he was leaving, my father asked, "What time can I see you tomorrow?"

"Didn't I tell you no?" the banker retorted. "Don't you come back here tomorrow!"

Dad, however, knew that God had spoken to him, and "no" from this man meant nothing to him when God was speaking. He spent the night in prayer.

Dad had a friend in town, a businessman whom he told about the exchange with the banker. He told the man he was going to see the banker again.

"You're a fool!" his friend said. "When the bank says no, they mean no. You'll get thrown out on your ear."

"If I do," my father replied, "I'll get up and walk back in again. 'No' does not mean anything when God is working."

He spent the morning in prayer, had lunch, then headed back toward the bank. Just as he approached the building, the banker happened to be coming back from his own lunch break.

"Well, hello!" my father said as he followed the banker through the front door.

"There you are again!" the banker cried. "I told you not to come back."

He looked my father in the eye. My father looked right back into his eyes.

"God was working," my father recalled later.

Suddenly, without another word, the banker sighed, "Come in and get the keys. I'm going to let you have that building free of charge, and you can fix it up to suit yourself."

My father resisted the urge to shout, "Glory, hallelujah!" but he certainly felt like it. He had his building, just as God had said.

In the days ahead, as my parents cleaned and renovated the space, they experienced miracle after miracle: free utilities, people paying them to carry off old stuff, and so on. They announced a citywide revival to inaugurate the new "Gospel Temple." The local paper donated nearly a full column of advertising each weekend. The revival ran two years and ten nights without skipping a night. They also had daily prayer meetings and a Bible study every afternoon. Hundreds were saved; scores were healed by the prayers of faith. Tourists visiting Hot Springs for its famous baths often attended services; one evening the congregation included people from thirty-eight states as well as Canada.

As the Depression deepened, my parents took in the needy. With eighteen rooms upstairs, we had so much space that we sometimes had as many as twenty guests. Somehow my mother always came up with meals for everybody, and she never turned down any of the hundreds of tramps who knocked at our door. More than once we were literally out of food and my parents would go to prayer, only to hear a knock at the door, with someone delivering food simply because God had directed them to.

THE TROUBLE WITH GOOD WORKS

It is remarkable to remember my parents' compassion for the poor since we were so poor ourselves. Sometimes we lived in downtown areas among gamblers and prostitutes. Once I watched from my window as a woman ran out of a building screaming. Another time I saw a man shoot another man; the victim fell and rolled under a car, and the man with the gun knelt to shoot his victim twice more. Some days we didn't have enough to eat, and in school my stomach would growl, to my great embarrassment. For some reason, I have never been able to forget the moment when my mother was ill, and my father could only provide for us by slicing up a head of cabbage and serving it to us raw.

In their enthusiasm for the work of God, my parents sometimes, as the old saying goes, bit off more than they could chew. They published and edited a church publication, which at one point had more than four thousand subscribers. At the same time, they operated a huge orphanage, three stories high. In addition to that, they issued credentials to more than two hundred fifty preachers, in practice laying the groundwork for a new denomination.

But the day came when they realized their workload was unrealistic. "We were so busy with good works," my father said, "that we failed in doing our best for the Lord." He went on, "Souls were going to hell while we were trying to carry on a good work."

So eventually they found private homes for the orphans, parceled out the orphanage facilities, and folded the publishing operation. As for the credentialing of ministers, my father observed with disgust that in every conference of these preachers the majority lobbied for the establishment of some kind of creed that would include some and exclude others. Throughout his lifetime, my father was opposed to "forming another sect." He refused to come up with "another butcher knife to cut up and divide God's people," or to "erect a chop block like the other sects had done, where they lead you up and cut your head off if you don't dance according to their music." He was determined to cooperate with all of God's children, difficult as that might be!

Ultimately, the preachers he had credentialed, supposedly as part of a group opposed to division and sectarianism, wore my father down. Their bickering over doctrinal details made his soul ache.

"I would rather dissolve the whole business and slip out in the back-woods and live on my knees and read my Bible and have the fire of God in my soul and be anointed by the Spirit of the Lord and commune with God and stay in touch with Him, and start all over from the bottom," he declared, "than to be a bishop or a leader of a great movement, at the same time all dried up in my soul, with no time to pray and commune with the Lord."

And that is just what he did.

A NEW AND DIFFERENT PERSON

Having been raised by a father who believed in working his children hard, my own father put us kids to work. He had seen other preachers' kids "idling," and the results weren't good. It occurred to him to get us started in music, since he loved music himself but had never had the opportunity to study it. He knew we had the potential to help him in ministry if we learned to play instruments and sing.

In the depths of the Depression, without much money at all, he went to a pawn shop and bought some stringed instruments on credit. He pro-duced a guitar and something called a banjo-guitar for me, mandolins for my sisters Ruth and Leona, and a standard banjo for my brother, Clement. My sister Mary was born mentally disabled and couldn't learn to play an instrument; our youngest sister Juanita was still too small. My father had also somehow acquired a piano, which he now traded for a good-quality saxophone, immediately taken up by Clem. (Later he was able to purchase an accordion, which my mother took a fancy to.)

Of course, as per my father's peculiar style of operation, we now had a load of instruments without a clue about how to play them—and no money to hire a teacher. My father, again as per his peculiar style of operation, went to prayer over the matter. Soon a knock came at the door. A music teacher from Chicago stood there; he was broke and needed to serve in a church in exchange for the freedom to advertise for private music students. He understood my father pastored the biggest church in town. My father welcomed him into the church and put his family up in some of our eighteen rooms over the church in trade for private lessons for us Humbard children. We got a top-quality start in our music education!

When the teacher and his family moved on just three months later, I was thirteen years old. I thought this was my opportunity to bail out. My father thought otherwise. To convince me to stick with my musical studies, he gave me a major whipping.

Neighbor kids came over, wanting to play, but every day after school we had to practice our music. On Saturdays we practiced our music. On Sunday afternoons we met in the "music room" above the church and practiced our music together. "You can go in and sit down and watch them," my parents offered to children who visited, "or go home."

I continued dogging it, learning nothing—until my father announced that I would appear on the platform at our church as a member of our family's musical group, with my brothers and sisters, during Sunday services beginning in thirty days, so I had better learn to play the guitar by then, or else.

I still stubbornly refused to practice, and when that dreaded Sunday arrived, I still hardly knew one musical note from another. The guitar on my lap felt as heavy as cement.

But a few days later, my life turned an incredible corner. I was sitting in our church, listening to a visiting evangelist preach the message of God, and suddenly I had the feeling that God Himself was speaking to me in the man's words and awakening in my heart for the first time a real and exciting belief in Jesus Christ. I had been born and raised in the Christian church, my parents were deeply religious, and I had attended church services almost every night of my entire life, but until that moment, I had never felt any deep belief in God. Now I suddenly realized that going to church and listening to other people would never make me believe in God. That was a decision that I had to make by myself in my own heart. At that moment, I decided that Christ was my Savior, and I felt gloriously happy. I listened to the preacher inviting new believers to come forward to the altar, and I felt the urge to answer his call. Still, I hesitated. God must have known I needed a little push, because a woman sitting nearby came across the aisle and whispered to me, "Are you saved?"

I got out of my seat and walked down the aisle, knelt there, and opened my heart to Jesus Christ. Right then and there, a new light flooded my soul; I became a new and different person. I decided that I would live for the Lord and give the rest of my life to His service. Whereas I had been shy and indifferent, I became instead a relaxed and happy young person, ready and eager to talk about God to anybody who would listen, anxious to do any kind of work—including the study of music—that might help our ministry. To my father's amazement, I was often the first one to jump up at our Bible meetings and give public testimony to my belief in God, something I would have been too embarrassed to do before, even if I had felt such an urge. It wouldn't be till several years later that I took actual Bible and religion courses and became ordained as a minister, but I truly became a minister as a thirteen-year-old that day at the altar.

IF GOD HAD A TENT

A few months later, the Ringling Bros. and Barnum & Bailey Circus came to Hot Springs. I couldn't attend. Not only did I not have money for a ticket, my parents were too strict about such "worldly" entertainment to allow me to go. But that didn't stop me from getting up at dawn, like all the other kids in our neighborhood, to see the elephants unloaded from the circus train and to watch the roustabouts putting up the huge big-top tent. I hung around the circus lot all day long and stayed on into the evening, sitting on a rail fence and watching the big crowds of people gathering to see the show.

I looked at the throngs surging into the magnificent, brightly lighted canvas arena, and I thought about my father preaching the Gospel under the small, tattered tents that we often used at rural meetings, when we couldn't rent a dingy hall or an empty theater on the back street of a nearby town. My parents had little concept of promotion; even though God often gave them large crowds, they were passive about advertising in order to build crowds. I was wired differently. I wanted to go where the people were and bring them in: "Go out into the highways and hedges, and compel them to come in, that my house may be filled," Jesus said in Luke 14:23; and those words burned in my spirit.

Watching the crowds pressing into the circus tent, I clenched my fists and pounded them together. "If God only had a big tent like that," I said to myself, "He'd have a crowd like that! If only we could get God's work out of the back alleys, and put it here on Main Street where it belongs!"

I promised myself that night to spend my life trying to put God on

Main Street. Little did that thirteen-year-old boy realize, on that June day in 1932, that someday, through the God-given gift of television, he would bring the teachings of the Bible to hundreds of millions of people all around the world.

But at the moment, there was no such thing. There was only radio!

THREE

Bait in the Water

As a new creature in Christ, I suddenly saw the potential for advancing our evangelistic work through music. Music could draw a crowd to hear the Gospel, and radio could take our music to multiplied thousands whom we could never reach in person or by conventional publicity methods.

I bought a chord book and practiced on my guitar for hours every day. I kicked myself for not paying attention to the lessons we had received from the music teacher. I took full charge of our little group, overseeing practices and running rehearsals. I drove my troupe relentlessly, sometimes till the wee hours of the morning. One night at 2:30 a.m. we were still going strong and my mother pleaded with my father to shut us down so she could get some sleep. "We had too hard a time getting them started," he replied. "I'm not going to interfere now. I'd rather move my sleeping place!"

I went to a local radio station to watch bands perform, then I came home and drilled my siblings in the musical techniques I had witnessed.

We placed a music stand in front of us as we played and sang, pretending that the stand was a radio microphone and we were performing for a radio audience.

"We've got to sound like professionals," I kept telling the others.

When we were barely ready, I went to the manager of local station KTHS, intent on persuading him to let us do one number on his two-hour Saturday evening country music program, *The Saturday Night Jamboree*, which was broadcast live from the city auditorium. This was radical, but my father had agreed to it because it might "change the spirit of things" if we offered a little Christian music in the midst of their worldly lineup. KTHS was a 10,000-watt station, reaching into thirty-three states.

The manager looked at me, skinny and only thirteen years old, with a guitar under my arm.

"I want to sing songs on the radio," I said. "My dad's running the church in the theater down there," I replied, gesturing in the proper direction, "and he doesn't have anybody to preach to. He's got a thousand seats, but on a Sunday morning he only has about forty people to speak to. If you let me sing on the radio and tell people where my dad is preaching, I'll get him a crowd."

It certainly wasn't the eloquence of my presentation that persuaded him; it had to be God! The manager took me into a little room. I had never seen a microphone before. "I'm going to turn that light on up there," the manager explained, "and when it comes on, you start talking and singing." I did as I was told. Desperate, I think, to fill his programming schedule, he invited us onto the program.

On our debut night, fifteen musical groups performed on the broadcast before we came on. We were something of a novelty, four young brothers and sisters singing and playing instruments. My sister Ruth took the lead on accordion, and we presented "The Old Rugged Cross."

44

It was clear before we had finished that the radio station's staff members were in shock. The station manager was yelling at me before we could get out the door.

"You kids double-crossed me," he shouted. "You know we don't allow Gospel songs on this program. If I had known you were going to do a religious number, I never would have let you go on the air." I don't know what he thought a preacher's kid was going to offer his radio audience if not Gospel content! But he was furious.

Ruth was crying as we returned home. We were all downhearted, but my mother responded calmly. "We'll pray over it," she said quietly, "and God will work it out."

A few days later, the station manager called me. He wanted us back, and he wanted "some more of that religious stuff." It turned out that *The Saturday Night Jamboree* had been dying, with virtually no listener response. But that week, they had received a record-shattering eighty-five letters of praise from listeners, sixty-three of which singled out the Humbard group, asking for more religious music.

It was the beginning of a new era for *The Saturday Night Jamboree*. The name was soon changed to *The Country Store*, and soon more than half of the airtime was dedicated to Christian music. Unlike many media managers, their listeners, the general public, appreciated music tuned to spiritual themes, and they responded warmly.

A year later, my dad's church had more than a thousand attending every week. It was my first experience pioneering in the territory beyond the walls of the church, in the "mission field" of the electronic media.

This was the beginning of a new era for the Humbard children, because we found that wherever we traveled in evangelism, radio generated a tremendous response. We began asking local radio stations to put us on the air wherever we went, and invariably their response rates exploded when we sang and played Gospel music. The novelty of a musical family opened the door, but the Spirit of God moving through the lyrics and the music did the rest. Multitudes came to our evangelistic meetings because they heard us on the radio. Countless thousands were saved in our meetings as the end result of our simple but unusual family act, coupled with the power of radio. Eventually KTHS gave us a Saturday morning Gospel music program of our own.

I came to believe early on that if you want to catch fish, you've got to have some bait. You just don't throw the hook in the water. You've got to get people's attention. Back in the early days of radio, ministers often went on the radio and just sat there and talked. They reached some, but they didn't reach people who weren't interested in just talk. I wanted to get past the "easy" audience, to people who wanted entertainment. I had no qualms about entertaining people with Gospel music; it was great bait! We tried to produce the best music possible, and we always had a message along with it, in hopes of reaching beyond the obvious audience of "church people" and into the wide reaches of a lost and dying world.

LED BY THE SPIRIT

As the Gospel Temple became more and more firmly established, my parents were led to travel the evangelistic circuit more and more. While most of the children in our family were of school age, we stayed in Hot Springs for the school year and spent the entire summer on the evangelistic circuit. The older we got, the more we were on the road. At one point we left for a thirty-day meeting in Georgia and didn't go home for more than two years, except for a couple brief visits.

As the first child to drive, I often chauffeured the family, leaving my father to "commune with the Lord and get the mind of God," as he put it. Sometimes this had troubling consequences. As we finished a series of meetings in Wooster, Ohio, my father felt led to go to a certain church in

Petersburg, Michigan. Unfortunately, a high church official had already been booked in the church, with advertising plastering the town. The church leaders politely declined my father's offer. He couldn't get peace about the matter, and wired them again. They sent another telegram, repeating the refusal. He was intent on going until we all ganged up on him, Mom included, and convinced him that he was being foolish.

Reluctantly, Dad told me to point the car south and head toward home. But within a hundred miles, he told me to pull the car to the side of the road. At first I thought he was sick.

"No, I am burdened," he said. "I fear that we are missing the Lord. Let's stop for a few minutes. I want to pray and have another talk together."

Soon he was saying, "Well, you better turn the car right around, and let's go to Petersburg."

We all began to argue with him, telling him how silly it was to go up there when they didn't want him.

"It ain't a question of whether they want us," he replied. "It's a question of whether the Lord wants us to go or not. Telegrams and letters and 'no' from people do not mean a thing to a man when God is leading differently."

My mother couldn't even convince him otherwise.

"Well, we're going," he finally said, "if we don't do anything but just say hello and turn around go back south. I don't want to carry this burden any longer."

So I dutifully turned the car around, and we headed for Michigan.

We arrived Tuesday evening; the well-publicized citywide revival would start Wednesday evening. We checked in with the local pastor (to my embarrassment), and he introduced us to his brother, a pastor from Toledo, who was visiting him. It turned out that the brother from Toledo was holding a revival that week, and he invited us to head back down to

Toledo, just twenty miles or so to the south, to minister there. We agreed, and along with the Petersburg pastor, we headed to Toledo. In the service, my mother and brother and sisters all sang and played our instruments, and the pastor graciously invited my father to preach. After the service, the Toledo pastor made my father an offer: "I want you to stay here awhile and help me in this revival."

"That would be a good idea!" his brother from Petersburg chimed in. "Maybe the Lord brought you up here just for that purpose."

But my father, again, to my embarrassment, was resolute.

"The Lord did not lead me at this time to come to Toledo," he insisted. "The Spirit of the Lord urged me to go to Petersburg. So I'm going back home with you tonight."

We all loaded up and went back up to Petersburg.

The Petersburg pastor was clearly troubled. He could see that my dad was making a mess of things.

But the next day dawned, and things changed. The pastor came rushing in, his face flushed. He had a telegram from the big shot who was supposed to launch the revival that night; illness had befallen the man's family and he would have to cancel. Could my father take his place?

Lesser men might have needled the poor pastor, but my father's face simply lit up. "Why, sure!" he exulted. "Praise the Lord! That's why the Lord told me to come up here. I knew we were going to have a revival!" The local pastor was so thrilled that my father had spurned his advice and come to town that he rented a house trailer, moved his family into it, and insisted that we Humbards live in his house throughout the revival!

Strange as it may seem, this was not an unusual occurrence with my father. He routinely heard one thing from people and another thing from God. Often people invited him—even sent him money for transportation—only to have him return the money and refuse the offer because God had told him to head elsewhere, and generally without a promise of a paycheck. Yet somehow, supernaturally, God always provided. To this day I believe it was because my father made it a habit to spend an amazing amount of time in prayer. "Don't try to go somewhere they don't want you," he admonished, "unless you have prayed through on it and are sure that the Spirit of the Lord is leading you. Otherwise you will get into trouble. I don't believe in pushing yourself and running over anybody, but being led of the Lord is more important than anything else." And then he would quote Romans 8:14: "For as many as are led by the Spirit of God, they are the sons of God." I honestly never knew of a person who put in as many hours in prayer as my father. Most people in our day would think of it as crazy, but it paid off for my father again and again in souls saved. And that, in the end, was all he ever really cared about anyway.

STRINGS ATTACHED

In our first decade as the "Humbard Family," we appeared on local radio stations from Texas to the Carolinas, from Georgia to Michigan, including Oklahoma, Arkansas, Ohio, Indiana, Pennsylvania, Tennessee, and beyond. By 1943 we were also receiving mail from listeners of ninety-one network stations all across the U.S. and Canada.

But God had even bigger things in store for us, and He had been laying plans from the time we were very young. Early in our musical ministry, a man came through Hot Springs from Chicago, heard us sing in the radio station, and made a point of speaking with me, as the eldest in the group. He was a talent scout for the *WLS Barn Dance*, a hugely popular country music radio show out of Chicago, and had an offer for us: one hundred dollars per child per week. This was an astounding amount of money at the time and would still be pretty impressive today! We were still in the depths of the Depression; money was painfully tight.

But I needed to know: what would he require of us?

"I'll put you on our 50,000-watt station every day," he said. "You can go ahead with your Gospel playing and singing."

This sounded good.

"But we'd also expect some hillbilly comedy numbers." He continued: "Love songs, ballads, maybe some jazz tunes. With a variety like that, you kids will make a great road-show unit, and that's where the real big money is."

I didn't need to think or pray about that; I didn't need to go home and ask my parents. I turned him down flat. Our only interest in music, I explained, was to spread the message of the Gospel. We would play and sing Christian songs only.

"I've never had anyone turn me down before," the man replied. "You're making a great mistake, sonny. You'll never get anywhere in this business unless you mix it up."

The man left, but that wasn't the last of him. The next day was Sunday, and I was astonished to see that talent scout sitting in the second row at our Gospel Temple. After the service, he approached my father.

"I just had to get a look at you folks," he said, "even if it meant getting myself to church for the first time in twenty years. I had to see what kind of people would raise children like these kids, who turn down big money on account of their religious convictions. You've got something here. And you put on a pretty good show in this church. Keep it up."

We did. And the some-strings-attached offers kept coming. A huge station offered us more money—five hundred dollars a week—but we had to add non-Christian songs to our lineup. We declined. Other similar offers came. As we grew more popular, the frequency of such offers increased. But nobody wanted us as we were. They wanted us to be a country music act that happened to do a lot of Christian music. So we said no, again and again.

In Cincinnati, the manager of the huge station WLW called me in. "I want to hire you as our special daily radio players," he said. "You can go ahead with your religious work and help your dad in meetings, and we will even make spot announcements during the day, telling where you'll be in religious services. I'll give you five hundred dollars a week, and gradually raise it along."

I was ready to go for it.

"This might be a pretty good thing," I responded, calculating in my mind. "We could work around here for a year or more, holding revivals."

But then I paused, and asked about his requirements.

"Just go ahead and play and sing your religious songs like you're doing," he assured me. "But add two or three other pieces, so we can please everybody."

I shook my head. "We couldn't do that, even if you gave us a thousand dollars a week," I answered. I explained our commitment to serve God with every breath in our bodies.

"Yes, but son, just look at the money you'll get!" the manager sputtered. "Look at the happiness it would bring to you youngsters to have so much money to spend."

"I disagree with you," I had to reply. "The only thing that brings happiness is to do the right thing and live right and love and serve the Lord. It's not money that makes people happy." Then I asked him, if money makes people happy, why do so many wealthy people commit suicide?

> The only thing that brings happiness is to do the right thing and live right and love and serve the Lord.

Maybe God had led me to hit a nerve with him. Tears welled in his eyes. "Rex, you've got something there," the man said quietly. "You're right." He sighed heavily. "I like your spunk. Stay with it, and you will reach your goal."

Word kept spreading. We were an unusual group, a talented group, and we would not compromise our values for money. The day would come when the nationwide Mutual Network would put us on the air free of charge. In November 1943, the vast Blue Network would pick us up, airing us five times a week, enabling us to reach people from Alaska to the Bahamas. Whenever my father talked about our "radio work," he simply smiled and quoted Matthew 6:33: "But seek ye first the kingdom of God, and his righteousness; and all these things shall be added unto you" (KJV). To him, it was as simple as that. God was telling the truth.

JUST A KID

We traveled more and more. We held evangelistic meetings literally coast to coast. My father preached; my mother took the pulpit once a week; we children sang and played our music. My father was often scorned as "that peculiar preacher," "old-fashioned," an "Arkansas hillbilly," an "old dreamer," "dangerous," "different." But we found if we could get someone in the door to a meeting, the ministry—our country-style Gospel music and his down-home Gospel preaching—was powerfully effective.

In town after town, we urged the city fathers to welcome us, to give us space, for their own benefit: a citywide revival would reach people that the churches couldn't, and this would make a better town. We talked to local pastors the same way: our meetings would draw people into their own church families after we had moved on. We saw it in hundreds of cities and towns, month after month and year after year; we knew it was true.

In those days, it was big news when a traveling musical family came to town, and this novelty established its own momentum. When people heard about it, they wanted to experience it. When they experienced it, God used it to lead them to Christ! Radio exposure dramatically multiplied the number of people who heard about the meetings. There's no telling how many more people were saved through the years who might otherwise never have heard the Gospel, simply because of our dogged determination to get on the radio everywhere we went. We witnessed the conversion of every imaginable type of person: drunks, gambling addicts, people on the verge of suicide, lawyers, doctors, bankers, businesspeople, teachers and school administrators and college professors, the list goes on. Evangelism was our sole calling; lost souls were our target, and we would do anything necessary—go to any length, try any experiment, pay any price—to reach them.

From the time I was thirteen, I handled the management of our family ministry. I arranged for auditoriums, sometimes facilities seating upwards of five thousand people. I was so young that facilities managers often disbelieved me. In Memphis, in the 1940s, I went in to book the six-thousand-seat Ellis Auditorium. I wanted to rent it for thirty days. The manager looked at me skeptically: "You're just a kid," he said. "What are you going to do with it?" I told him about our ministry. He couldn't believe it. Finally I asked him to call the National Auditorium Association of America and ask about me. Yes, they told him, I had rented their auditoriums in various locations; we'd paid the rent and everything was fine. Soon after that I asked the Association to give me a letter certifying my legitimacy so I wouldn't have to argue with facilities managers in other cities!

LOVE AT FIRST SIGHT

In the winter of 1937, America prepared to celebrate President Franklin Roosevelt's birthday with big March of Dimes shows benefiting polio research all over the nation. We were astonished and delighted to be invited to perform in the Dallas show. A prominent music publisher and producer of concerts and radio shows, V. O. Stamps of the Stamps–Baxter

Music and Printing Company, was staging the Dallas event, and we were among the many popular musicians that Stamps selected to appear. It was such an honor that our whole family, including the youngest girls, Mary and three-year-old Juanita, packed up and drove to Dallas for the gala occasion.

Backstage at the auditorium on the night of the show, when it was almost time for the Humbards to go onstage, I was holding Juanita by the hand, trying to keep her quiet, when I found myself gazing into the dark eyes of one of the most attractive girls I had ever seen. And those eyes were staring deeply back at me. My siblings were beckoning me onstage, but I had to meet this girl. What if she was gone by the time we finished our act? Thinking fast, I led Juanita to the dark-eyed girl, who was evidently a singer in a trio, because two other girls were with her. "If you're not going onstage right away," I said, "would you mind keeping an eye on my baby sister while we sing our number?"

To my great relief she said, "I'll be glad to."

I picked up my guitar and hurried onstage, knowing that I had trapped the girl with my baby sister until I could return and get her name and address. "Thank you, God," I prayed silently.

The huge audience responded thunderously to our rendition of the old Gospel song "Meeting in the Air." But I wasn't thinking about any of that as I rushed offstage; I wanted to see the angel who was minding Juanita. My path was blocked, however, by the enthusiastic pastor of Dallas's Bethel Temple, Rev. Albert Ott.

"Now just hold up a minute, son," he said. "Everybody here is very much impressed by the talent of your group. How about appearing on our church's radio program tomorrow morning?"

I told him we would be glad to. I would have given him anything, anything at all, just to get past him, to get back to Juanita's babysitter! I could see her smiling at me from the far edge of the backstage crowd.

When I finally reached her and took my little sister off her hands, I found myself tongue-tied. But Rev. Ott was still beside me talking about his plans for using us on his radio program, and suddenly I heard him say, "Oh, you already know Maude Aimee?"

"Well, not really," I stammered, "but I sure would like to!"

So Rev. Ott proceeded to introduce me to Maude Aimee Jones and to advise her that he was hoping, not only to put us on his program the next morning, but to bring us onto the staff of his church.

"Maude Aimee and her family," he added, "are parishioners of our church."

God works in wonderful ways! When we arrived at the church the next morning to appear on the Bethel Temple program, we learned to my great delight that Ott and Stamps had worked out a plan that would keep the whole Humbard family in Dallas for the next *two years*. At the time, Bethel Temple was one of the largest churches in the country, with more than a thousand youngsters in its Sunday school program and a busy evangelistic ministry that was spreading the Word of God through thirteen radio programs a week. Rev. Ott wanted the Humbard youngsters to provide Gospel music on all of these radio programs and to work at the Temple, where my father would also serve as an assistant pastor. At the same time, my brother and sisters would appear on Stamps's radio programs and in concerts he was staging all over that part of Texas. Twenty programs a week! Stamps would also give us free lessons through his two music schools in Dallas, provide our family with living quarters on the third floor of the church plus living expenses, a Ford automobile, and a weekly allowance of spending money! All of this and Maude Aimee Jones, too! It was incredible!

My family members weren't as enthusiastic as I was. They weren't in love, I guess. But I pitched them hard.

"There's only 35,000 people in the entire county back in Hot Springs,

Arkansas," I said. "We'll never go anywhere or do anything for God just being in Hot Springs. We'd better take this opportunity. We can reach more souls if we can get this exposure."

They finally caved in to my arguments, and we headed back to pack out of Hot Springs. Our family friend John Hendricks, who would later marry my sister Leona's mother-in-law and still later join our staff at the Cathedral of Tomorrow in Akron, Ohio, stepped up to serve as pastor of our church in Arkansas. Pastor Ott at Bethel Temple arranged for our transfer from high school in Hot Springs, where I was midway through my senior year.

I moved to Adamson High School in Dallas, where the principal granted us special permission to come in late every morning so we could appear on Bethel Temple's daily early-morning radio broadcasts. Later, on high school graduation day, my fellow Adamson High band members blew their horns as I walked across the stage to receive a diploma that had come from Hot Springs High. As part of the ceremony, the Stamps Quartet and the Humbard Family sang in an open field with an enormous sound system mounted on a flatbed truck. More than ten thousand were in attendance.

During the next two busy but wonderfully exciting years, we usually appeared on as many as twenty-eight radio programs a week, plus two Sunday services and one Wednesday evening service at Bethel Temple. Our schoolwork and music lessons at the Stamps music schools were sandwiched between trips ranging from 50 to 500 miles one way, which took us to concerts and recitals where we appeared with the famed Stamps Quartet. We often returned from a Stamps Quartet event at daylight, went straight to the studio for the morning program, and then went directly to school!

And yet all of this was dull background to me, because I was getting to know Miss Maude Aimee Jones, the girl I had fallen in love with at first sight that night backstage at the State Fair Grounds Auditorium.

Maude Aimee was only fifteen when I met her; I was eighteen. I was her first boyfriend; she was my first and only girlfriend. Years later she would refer to me as "a slow Arkansas traveler" because it took me six months to ask her to "go steady." But I was sold from day one.

Our mutual faith in Jesus Christ was a strong bond between us. Maude Aimee was the devoutly religious daughter of a devoutly religious mother, Maude Jones. Maude's home in Dallas was a haven for visiting evangelists, including the renowned Aimee Semple McPherson, a close friend for whom Maude Aimee was named. There were always a few preachers from out of town at Mrs. Jones's plentiful dinner table. Her church was the center of her life and the lives of her two children, Maude Aimee and Charles. Charles was eleven years older than his sister and already married to Rev. Ott's daughter Aretes.

Maude Aimee and her mother went to church whenever the doors were open: all day on Sunday, Wednesday evenings, and to meetings and special services on other days and nights, too. Maude Aimee came forward to accept Christ under the ministry of her pastor, Rev. Ott, when she was just six years old, a tribute to her mother's guidance and to her pastor's ability to express the Gospel so clearly that even a small child could understand it. When Maude Aimee was eight, she was singing Gospel songs at Sunday services and revival meetings and on the Temple's radio programs.

I was allowed to court Maude Aimee before her sixteenth birthday only because I came from a similarly strict religious family. Mrs. Jones had been left alone to rear her two children when Maude Aimee was only fifteen months old, so she was more protective of her daughter than she might have been if there were a husband and father to share the responsibility. As a teen, Maude Aimee had never been allowed to stay overnight at a girlfriend's house, nor had she ever seen a football or basketball game. It was a big event in her life when her mother finally gave me permission to take her to a football game at the Cotton Bowl. "I'm allowing this only because you're a fine Christian young man," Mrs. Jones told me.

On our dates and on my many visits to Maude Aimee's home, we were always chaperoned. Keeping the two of us under observation kept Mrs. Jones mighty busy, because I was at her house every day waiting for Maude Aimee to come home from her job at Franklin's, one of the biggest women's wear stores in Dallas, where she went to work as a salesperson soon after she turned sixteen. Next to her church work and her Gospel singing, Maude Aimee's main interest was fashionable clothes. She soon left her selling job at Franklin's to become the decorator of the store's display windows and a manager of its fashion shows.

It was after we had been keeping company for almost two years that I was finally able to gather my courage and say to her, "Maude Aimee, I need you for my life partner. In fact, I've just got to have you."

Her startling reply had an eloquent simplicity: "Okay, Rex."

A few days after, on Christmas Eve, I handed her a large box, about three feet square and two feet deep, beautifully gift wrapped. She unwrapped the box and then unwrapped three others inside it, each one smaller than the previous one, until she came to a tiny package with a note inside: "Look inside the other box." I pulled "the other box" out of my pocket. Inside it was her engagement ring.

Maude Aimee's mother and my parents felt we were still too young to take on the responsibilities of marriage. She was seventeen and I was twenty. So we agreed to wait until I was more firmly established in the service of God that would be our life's work. Waiting meant a long separation, because my father had accepted a call to a church in Little Rock, where he would need my help in organizing his meetings and promoting them on radio broadcasts. Maude Aimee and I tried to convince each other, without much enthusiasm, that carrying on our romance through the mail and long-distance telephone calls for the next year or more would really test and strengthen our love. As things turned out, we were to be apart for more than two and a half years.

On the gloomy day when we said good-bye and I headed the Humbard family car out of Dallas, I was so downcast and moody that I drove the first eighty-five miles without noticing that I was still in second gear. My family felt so sorry for me that none of them wanted to point out my error. During my first few weeks in Little Rock, I made more phone calls to Dallas than I could afford, and I flooded Maude Aimee's mailbox with letters. One day I wrote eight letters to her, one of them twenty-five pages long.

I tried to distract myself by working hard buying time on local radio stations for our Gospel music to promote Dad's church services and tent revival meetings and then scurrying all over town to persuade sponsors to reimburse us. We did a live broadcast every morning at 6:15, seven days a week, before Clement and Leona went off to their high school classes. We also did an hour-long broadcast on Thursday nights that drew mail from thirty-three states and some Canadian provinces. Preparing for the day when I would become a minister with a congregation that might help me to support a wife, I took an active role in conducting our church's services, acting as the master of ceremonies, giving the welcoming talk, leading prayers and songs, and introducing my father. At the end of his message, I stood up again to invite people to come forward and receive Christ as Savior. This detail—encouraging people to accept Christ by making a public profession of faith—gave me valuable experience in the most important single function of an evangelist. But it was more than just a skill enabling me to perform a function; I began to understand that it was a God-given gift, a kind of "anointing" that God used to draw people to faith in Christ. I couldn't explain it; I still can't. It's just something He decided to use me for, and I am grateful.

THE POWER OF LOVE

My father, still ministering as part of Pastor Ott's staff, managed to run afoul of the church's denomination for officiating at the wedding of a preacher whose first wife had left him. Ott was already unpopular with his denominational leaders—the Otts were called "the Neiman Marcus Christians" because they dressed well—and this violation of the denomination's conservative code was an opportunity for the bureaucrats to pressure Pastor Ott. He could fire my father, or he could resign his credentials with the denomination.

As my family's manager, I was the one to sit down and hash it out with the pastor. I didn't like the choices.

"I don't want you to have to leave your brothers in the denomination," I told Pastor Ott. "We'll pick up and go."

The pastor objected. He was willing to resign his credentials, but I had decided on what I considered to be an honorable course of action. And we moved on, heading not back to Hot Springs, but to the much larger city of Little Rock.

In our relatively short time at Bethel Temple in Dallas, I had learned much from Albert Ott. Later, I would realize that I learned more from Pastor Ott than from any other individual in my life. I saw him do an early version of broadcast sponsorship; he had me make on-air announcements like, "Today's program has been made possible through the courtesy of McDormand Jewelry, and when you patronize them, you're helping a friend who has helped us." I also saw him stand at the front door of his church and shake hands with everybody who came through. He had one of the largest Sunday schools in the nation. His auditorium, with more than a thousand seats, was packed even for the midweek Wednesday evening services. People responded to the fact that he simply loved them. He never preached a big, eloquent sermon. He was just an edifier. He prayed with people. He cried with people. Sometimes in the middle of his sermon he would begin to weep with emotion; the altars would fill with people who felt the tug of God's Spirit in their hearts. From Albert Ott, I learned the power of love.

DISASTER

In Little Rock, as we prepared for the next phase of our family ministry, I thought back to the approach I had observed in the ministry of Aimee Semple McPherson in the days of my childhood. She had been a major figure nationwide, and an enterprising advertising agency had made her a unique proposition. They would pay her a fee to hold a crusade meeting in each city around the country; she could preach and pray and sing and whatever she wanted. The agency, on the other hand, would promote the meetings and, instead of receiving an offering, would sell tickets for admission. I remembered her coming to Hot Springs, to the three-thousand-seat auditorium where we appeared on the weekly *Country Store* radio program each Saturday evening. My parents wanted to experience her ministry, but because it cost money to get in, and we were painfully poor, they could bring only me, the oldest of their children. Aimee Semple McPherson had "gone commercial," and it didn't go down too well with poor rural folks.

But her approach did have advantages, and I wanted to replicate some of them. I made arrangements with radio stations in Hot Springs, Pine Bluff, and Little Rock, building a small statewide network. My family and I appeared on one network of stations at 6:30 a.m. each morning for half an hour, finishing with "Look Away to Jesus" as our theme song. A second network of stations agreed to pick us up beginning at 7:00 a.m., opening the program with the same song that was simultaneously concluding the previous program. When we finally finished at 7:30, we

61

packed up our instruments and the younger children headed off to school!

* * *

But then...disaster.

When someone told Maude Aimee, in error, that I was seeing someone else, she horrified me by breaking our engagement. It would take a year of prayer and maneuvering to get the relationship straightened out.

In the meantime, I was lost, bereft, grieving. But the work of reaching souls had to go on.

GIVE YOUR GAS STAMPS

When the famed evangelist Aimee Semple McPherson died, her son Dr. Ralph McPherson tried to carry on her ministry in Los Angeles by reading his mother's sermons. But he clearly wasn't the gifted preacher she had been, and soon he called us for help. Their Angeles Temple had fifty-five hundred seats, but he was having trouble filling them. He had seen the Humbards at a conference sometime before, and he wondered if we would hold a series of meetings to help him rebuild the ministry. We said yes.

The Angeles Temple organization also owned a radio station, so we broadcast our services each evening from the facility. Night after night we watched God at work filling the auditorium with people. Some nights we turned people away. Over those six highly successful weeks, we saw the Hollywood crowd and people from the music industry get interested in what we were doing. A young composer named Ralph Carmichael showed up one evening; he told me years later that he was shocked to see a guitar, a banjo, a mandolin, and a bass fiddle in church. But of course, the novelty thrilled him, and Ralph went on to become one of the greatest innovators in the entire Christian music world. God used us to show him that things didn't have to be done the old-fashioned way!

* * *

Jackie Burris was a hugely popular Baptist evangelist in those days, and he arranged to hold a month of meetings at Little Rock's Robinson Auditorium. The place was packed, running over with people, and I, of course, found a way to introduce myself to him. I had an offer for him to consider: we would play thirty minutes of music to warm up the crowd each evening before his service began. Burris loved the idea. We began at 7:00 p.m., with my family singing and me talking a bit, and the crowds loved us. When Burris's thirty-day crusade ended, he invited us to do the next date with him; he had staff musicians, but they didn't do country-style music. He was heading to the ten-thousand-seat Cadle Tabernacle in Indianapolis. We went—the place was packed four weeks in a row—then accompanied him to Cincinnati, South Bend, and Tulsa.

Back home in Little Rock, I shared a new idea with my family.

"Let's go back to Indianapolis," I said, "to Cadle Tabernacle. I believe we can fill it just like Burris did."

From our home base in Little Rock, I rented the Indianapolis facility. We printed posters and arranged to have them put on every trash can and bus in town, and we ran newspaper ads. I made a deal with the radio station to broadcast twice a day. But after all of this, as our departure date arrived, we were broke!

Those were the days of gasoline rationing, and we had a number of vehicles (including a house trailer) to get up to Indianapolis, so I asked our Little Rock congregation to give not only cash but also gas stamps. I took all the spare tires out of our vehicles and sold them. Finally we were able to get to Indianapolis.

Our campaign, like Jackie Burris's, was a huge success, and it was our first ministry in a ten-thousand-seat facility. But it was still the Depression, and offerings were meager. It was typical to pass the plate among eight thousand people and receive an offering of two hundred dollars. The builder of the Tabernacle, E. Howard Cadle, for whom it was named, decided to help. Each Sunday evening of our campaign, he would appear and make a statement to the crowd: "I like these meetings that the Humbards are holding. But folks, we've got to pay the rent for the week. Now I'm standing here with my checkbook. I want you to get up out of your seat and come down here and put an offering in the plate right here on the edge of the stage. Then I want the ushers to come down here and count it. When they get through, I'll write a check for the same amount that you folks give." That generous "matching challenge" strategy enabled us to pay our expenses throughout the campaign!

Something Called Television

It was in Indianapolis that the manager of the radio station on which we were broadcasting twice a day first mentioned something called television. He owned the license for the CBS station in the city; he was preparing to put the station on the air, and he wanted us to appear. There were hardly any television sets anywhere, but the manager needed programming, particularly on opening day.

We agreed. We showed up at the studio, waited for the initial fifteen-minute news program to finish, then sang our Gospel music. It was our first time on TV, the second-ever program to appear on the CBS-TV station in Indianapolis. Something inside me said, *This will be the next big thing.* When the state fair opened, the station's crew covered it, and we broadcast from the fair. I began to sense what God could do if we were able to minister regularly on television…and if more and more people owned TV sets! It's very possible that we had more people in our live audience at the fair than in our television audience across the region, with so few people owning television sets; but my appetite for reaching people with sound *and* pictures had been whetted. And our television ministry, after a fashion, had begun.

"YES, DARLING"

And it was there in Indianapolis that God—smiling on me—gave me my breakthrough with Maude Aimee.

A letter arrived from Maude Aimee's mother. I think my own mother was conspiring with her, since they could both see that their children were miserable being apart. My mother invited Maude Aimee to visit, and arrangements were made. Maude Aimee got on a train in Dallas, bound for Indianapolis, having sent a telegram advising us of her arrival. She knew I'd want to meet her at the station.

Unfortunately, I didn't get the telegram. Maude Aimee arrived, found no one at the station to pick her up (I confess at that moment I was actually playing doubles tennis with a young man and two young ladies), and she began fuming. She was seriously considering getting on the next train to Dallas when she finally decided not to squander the investment of all that travel. The letter from my mother had a return address, and she took a cab there.

My mother assured her that we had never received any telegram. In fact, it did arrive the next day, and Maude Aimee decided to let me off the hook for my failure. She sang in our meetings, and people responded warmly to her.

I saw my opportunity. I wasn't going to take the chance of losing her again. "How about marrying me this week?" I asked.

"Yes, darling," she replied. "This week."

I could hardly believe my ears. I thought she would want to go back to Dallas to have a nice wedding in her own church, with Rev. Ott performing the ceremony, as she had so often dreamed and talked about. But now she was too practical for that.

"We can't afford to go clear back to Texas right now and have a big wedding," she said. "We don't have that kind of money, and we're going to need every dollar we have to live on. Let's just ask your father to marry us in a simple little ceremony. We won't tell my mother or my brother about it until after we're married, because it would be too hard on them to come up here for the wedding."

I paid five dollars for a marriage license. When we went for the blood test, Maude Aimee was shocked to find that Indiana law differed from Texas law: the bride as well as the groom had to give blood! But she survived, so we got a ring and she chose a dress.

The "simple little ceremony" took place before a crowd of 8,500 people. After our final Sunday evening service at Cadle Tabernacle on August 2, 1942, I made an announcement: "Folks, there's going to be a wedding here immediately after the close of the meeting. If anyone wants to stay, you're welcome."

Nobody left! So Maude Aimee, looking beautiful in a light blue dress, took her place beside me on the platform, with my sister Ruth and her minister husband, Louis Davidson, standing by as our attendants. Dad led us in reciting our marriage vows and pronounced us man and wife, and I was so excited that I forgot to kiss the bride.

And I forgot something else. We had a big, long automobile of some kind, which family and friends had tied tin cans to. After the ceremony, Maude Aimee and I headed toward the Claypool Hotel in downtown Indianapolis. We were noisy going down the street, and soon a policeman pulled us over. "Young man, it's all right to get married and tie tin

cans on your car," he advised me solemnly, "but please turn your head-
lights on; you're going to get killed."

From the front desk of the hotel, we sent a telegram to Maude Aimee's
mother and brother back in Dallas. That was all it took to tip off the
hotel staff, and within a few minutes a porter arrived at our door with ice
water and champagne.

* * *

Two days later we were renting our first home: three rooms on the second
floor of an old house in South Bend, Indiana, where we were opening a
Gospel meeting in a tent. It was the beginning of ten rough years on the
road. We raised our two first boys driving from town to town, pulling a
small trailer home behind us, worrying about our threadbare tires and
where to find wartime-rationed gasoline, often wondering where our
next meal would come from. In some places where we drew large crowds,
the collection was so small that we had to sell one
of our family's automobiles to pay our bills before
leaving town.

Maude Aimee had given up a lot. Her work in
fashion merchandising had been satisfying and
glamorous. She sacrificed everything to take on
the hardships and uncertainties of living on the
road with a homeless traveling evangelist.

"Oh, it wasn't all that hard," Maude Aimee
insisted years later when an interviewer asked her
about those early years. "I enjoyed my job in
Dallas, and I loved working with stylish clothes,
but I wasn't carried away by it. I was raised to believe very strongly and

> She sacrificed
> everything to
> take on the
> hardships and
> uncertainties
> of living on
> the road with
> a homeless
> traveling
> evangelist.

deeply in what Rex was doing, and I felt that a man who was giving up comfortable security to work for God was just the man for me. Oh sure, there were times when I had to bring my wristwatch to a pawnshop for a little money to buy food for our children. But we always felt when the going was tough that God would never let us down, because we were doing His work. He never did let us down, and He never will."

FOUR

Love on the Road

$\mathcal{W}$e were pioneers. We blazed new trails; we lived "close to the ground"; we were always looking for the best way to reach lost people with the good news about Jesus. And Maude Aimee pioneered right along with us.

When she left her home in Dallas to visit me in Indianapolis, to see if our relationship had a future, she expected to be home again with her mother the following week and back at her department store job on Monday. Instead, she didn't see her hometown again till almost three months later. When we finally managed to get three days off from a revival meeting in Tulsa, we flew to a combined bridal shower and belated wedding reception at Bethel Temple, attended by more than two hundred people. Maude Aimee promised her mother and friends that she would see them at Christmas, but the two of us spent Christmas Eve alone atop Lookout Mountain in Tennessee. We were driving from Little Rock to Augusta, Georgia, where we had to get things ready for another evangelistic campaign, which would begin on New Year's Day. Such was

69

the life of a traveling evangelist's wife, but Maude Aimee claimed to love it...and appeared to!

We traveled; we preached; we sang; we prayed; we cried; we traveled some more. In a single year we hauled our house trailer from Vancouver to Miami and from New York City to Los Angeles. We sledge-hammered enough tent stakes into the ground that I eventually, out of exhaustion and desperation, designed a mechanical stake driver and had a Memphis company manufacture it for us. Anything to make the work simpler and the ministry more efficient for the sake of reaching more people!

My own ministry expanded; I had already been preaching one sermon a week for some years, substituting for my father. During a campaign in Greenville, South Carolina, I was ordained as a minister of the Gospel by the International Ministerial Federation, an organization of interdenominational clergy. For the first time, I was officially "Rev. Rex Humbard." It felt strange at first, but it felt right.

During that same Greenville campaign, we learned that Maude Aimee was pregnant. It was thrilling news, except for the fact that the doctor told her to avoid extra work. Maude Aimee was deeply dedicated to "doing her share" for the ministry. Perhaps to compensate, Maude Aimee began urging me to get her an instrument and let her learn to play. "If I could learn to play a musical instrument like the rest of you, I'd be much happier," she told me, "and more use to the Lord, too. I've been singing Gospel songs as long as I can remember, but I want to do something else during the services."

"Choose any instrument you please, honey," I replied.

I lived to regret that invitation. She chose the vibraharp. Many times, as I lugged that large, unwieldy contraption into an auditorium, I wished I had suggested the flute or the violin, something she could carry around herself, even while pregnant!

Trying to teach her to play the thing was an interesting challenge too, since I discovered to my surprise that my splendid vocalist-wife couldn't read a note of music. She had a great natural voice and a sharp ear; that's all. Maude Aimee would look at a sheet of music only to memorize the words, which she did quickly and easily. Still, within a week she had figured out the vibraharp, and was soon playing solo passages like a veteran.

We kept traveling, from South Carolina to North Carolina to Kentucky, until the due date was near. Maude Aimee wanted to be near her mother when the baby arrived, so she went to Dallas alone while I staged another meeting in Bowling Green, then joined her a week before the scheduled arrival. We were shopping for a trailer home when she suggested it was time to head to the hospital. The next morning at 5:55, we had a healthy ten-pound son: Alpha Rex Emmanuel Humbard, Jr.

The next day I made arrangements to buy the small trailer home that Maude Aimee had picked out for us, a little sixteen-foot Airstream Spartan, with a tiny living room, a bedroom, and a kitchen the size of a postage stamp, with a butane gas heater and a cooking stove. Acquiring a trailer had become crucial; it was getting almost impossible to find rooms for rent when we traveled, and adding a baby to the picture wasn't going to make it any easier. As the parents of an infant, we couldn't take the chance of being stranded on the road without a roof over our heads. Rex Jr. was on the road within weeks of his arrival, the newest pioneer in our family.

WRONG OFFICE, WRONG MAN

The road was hard enough, but finances were extremely tight, which added to the stress. When we blew a tire, repair or replacement might have to wait until we could scrape enough money together. When we pulled away from Dallas with our weeks-old son, I was still wondering how we were going to pay for our new trailer home.

But God, as usual, was working ahead of us.

At our next stop, in Nashville, I discovered that the program director of local radio station WSIX was an old friend of our family, Jack Woliver. He had given us our start in radio, back in Hot Springs. Jack arranged for us to perform on two of his daily radio programs, free of charge, to promote our meetings at the Dixie Auditorium.

After three weeks of these broadcasts, however, the station manager decided we weren't attracting enough listeners. He told Jack to notify us that our programs would be canceled.

Jack and I hastily cooked up a plan to prove to the manager that his estimate of our audience was too low. We printed a postcard featuring a photo of the Humbard Family Gospel music group. The next day, on both our morning and afternoon broadcasts, we offered to send the photo free to anybody writing to request it. Twelve hours later, we received 4,982 requests in the mail. By the end of the next day we had more than 8,200 written requests from our listeners.

We stayed on the air.

The strong response made waves, too. The Mutual Network got wind of this unusual new group and arranged to give us five radio programs a week on a "sustaining" basis. This meant that we received no money, but we were nonetheless delighted because we would gain nationwide promotion for our evangelist meetings.

After we left Nashville, we got bad news. The Mutual Network was canceling two of the programs, leaving us with three radio shows a week. Others might have been grateful just to have three exposures a week on such a big network, but something didn't set right with me. As I prayed about the matter, I sensed God leading me to go to New York—in spite of a serious shortage of funds—and not only try to get back on a five-day-a-week schedule, but also to get a salary. It didn't make logical sense, but as my father so often said, "no" doesn't mean "no" when God is saying "yes."

I didn't prepare a fancy sales talk; I just trusted God to lead me. In New York I went to see the Mutual Network executives, who flatly refused to give me five coast-to-coast broadcasts a week. I was lucky to get three sustaining programs, they advised me; and I couldn't disagree, except that God was stirring my spirit to keep asking. So I went to the NBC offices in Rockefeller Center and asked to see the program director for NBC's Blue Network.

"Which program director?" the receptionist asked. "We have five of them."

I searched in my briefcase for a paper with the name of an NBC man that Jack Woliver had suggested, but I had stupidly left it behind in my hotel room. I asked the receptionist for a list of the program directors, hoping that one of the names might look familiar, but I didn't recognize any. Taking a chance, I arbitrarily chose the name at the top.

"Charles Barry," I said. "I'd like to see Charles Barry."

I was led down a long carpeted corridor to Mr. Barry's office. He was sitting behind a desk.

"Mr. Barry, a mutual friend of ours, Jack Woliver in Nashville, Tennessee, suggested I should come here to see you."

Barry grinned. "I don't know anybody named Woliver," he replied. "Sit down and tell me what's on your mind."

I was obviously in the wrong office, talking to the wrong man. Praying silently and fervently, I began to talk about our Gospel music program and how much we wanted to put it on the radio from coast to coast five days a week. Barry had never heard of the Humbard Family. Did I have a recording of our music? he asked. I pulled a record from my briefcase: Columbia Records had released our country-rhythm rendition of "Christ Is Keeping My Soul."

He put it on a phonograph player, listened to it all the way through, then reset the needle to the beginning. He picked up the telephone, said to a sales manager, "Could we sell this?" and held the phone to the phonograph. After a few moments, they spoke again, then Barry hung up and turned back to me.

"What else do you do?"

"Well, I give inspirational talks," I responded, avoiding the word *sermons*. "And I recite poems."

"What kind of poems?"

I couldn't offer a description; I just began reciting the touching old poem "Flowers."

Barry's eyes had welled with tears. He stood up. "I'll take it," he said. "I'll have a hard time selling it to my boss; he's probably the man you came here to see. If you had gone to him, he wouldn't even have listened to the record. But I'll take it."

God had led me to the wrong office, to the wrong man, knowing that the "right office" and the "right man" would have been wrong! Charles Barry offered us a one-year contract to broadcast our program on NBC's Blue Network from coast to coast. No Gospel program had ever aired on NBC. And he offered to pay us the unthinkable sum of four hundred dollars a week. That would give us enough extra money to buy the trailer homes, automobiles, and sound equipment that our ministry desperately needed. In the months ahead, we broadcast from the various cities where we were holding our revival meetings, eventually expanding our coverage into Canada and onto Armed Forces Radio. We received letters from ships at sea and military bases all around the globe, thanking us for bringing the ministry to them as they served our country far from home. And it was often our network radio checks that paid for our food and basic living expenses when collections were low. Finding such riches, particularly in those days, was the equivalent of Peter, in Matthew 17:27, finding a coin in the fish's mouth to pay the disciples' taxes!

At the end of the one-year contract, the network wanted to attach a sponsor to us in order to offset their expenses in broadcasting our pro-grams. That would have been fine, but they insisted on our selling Carter's Little Liver Pills, which would have somewhat complicated our message that Jesus heals! It seems no other sponsors were lined up wait-ing to advertise on the Humbard Family programs, so NBC found a dif-ferent program, Arthur Fiedler and the Boston Pops, to attach to the sponsor. Our career as nationwide radio performers was brief, but the support had been perfectly timed for one of the neediest and most cru-cial seasons of our ministry.

Perfect Now

We were holding meetings in Detroit when we were slammed by terrible news: Rex Jr. was suffering from advanced tuberculosis.

Our world shattered. The x-rays were horrifying: two-thirds of his lungs had collapsed from infection. He was put to bed and given peni-cillin every two hours around the clock. Doctors urged us to place him as soon as possible in a sanitarium. We prayed desperately for God to help us, but our son's condition failed to improve.

Maude Aimee phoned her brother Charles Jones, a longtime pastor in Dallas, and asked him to pray. He was willing, but he also had a suggestion.

"Why don't you take him to Oral Roberts?"

"Who is Oral Roberts?" Maude Aimee asked.

Charles explained that Oral was an evangelist from Tulsa with a strong belief in the power of prayer to heal physical illness. Oral had suf-fered from TB in his youth, Charles added, so he was especially sympa-thetic to people afflicted with that disease.

We learned that Oral Roberts was about to open a tent meeting in Mobile. Could we drive Rex Jr. there? Too long a trip, the doctor said. We should take him to a sanitarium, he insisted. Finally, after assuring him that we would make the trip in leisurely stages with plenty of rest stops, the doctor gave us a green light to take our son to Alabama.

When we arrived, Oral was expecting us; Charles had told him of our situation. We led Rex Jr. to him. First, the evangelist prayed for Maude Aimee and me, asking God to bless our work as servants of His. Then, placing his hands on Rex Jr., he asked God very simply to heal the boy. Turning to us, he said, "Go now, and don't worry. The Lord has done the job."

The words of God to the prophet in Jeremiah 32:27 flashed through my mind: "Behold, I am the LORD, the God of all flesh: is there any thing too hard for me?" (KJV).

We stayed on for Oral's services, and Maude Aimee and I were both deeply refreshed by them. It was the first time we had attended any Christian services outside of our own ministry since before our wedding, and it was great to be on the "receiving end" for a change, taking in the nourishment of God's Word instead of working to give it out to other people. When we learned that Oral was planning to launch a new series of meetings in Tampa, we decided to follow.

By the time we got there, Rex Jr. had stopped coughing. His appetite had improved; he was putting on weight. In Tampa, Maude Aimee took Rex Jr. to another physician and asked to have his lungs examined. She had his previous x-rays in her bag, but she told the doctor nothing about our son's condition. The doctor examined his chest and x-rayed his lungs.

There was nothing wrong with him.

"Why did you bring this child here?" the doctor asked.

Maude Aimee pulled out the previous x-rays. The doctor was astounded. He took additional x-rays of Rex Jr.'s lungs and gave him a fluoroscopic examination as well.

"The child's lungs are now perfect," he said. "There's no scar tissue on either lung, and no sign of infection."

Still stunned, the doctor peered at the previous x-rays again.

"It's impossible for us to restore a lung as collapsed as this," he said, "and it could never be inflated again with this much damage in it. Your boy must have been cured by a Higher Power."

We rejoiced; we praised God. We watched our son continue to eat, a pattern he maintains to this day, and we began an abiding friendship with the great minister Oral Roberts. His ministry has been an inspiration to us and to multitudes down through the years, but we will always be especially grateful to God for the way He used Oral to spare our son.

IF I COULD PLAN PROBLEMS

During the next eight years, our family team traveled all over the United States and Canada. We even ministered to Indians and to Eskimos in Alaska. My brother Clement's new bride, Priscilla, joined our musical group. When my sister Leona married Wayne Jones, he gave up his promising career in aviation to work with us. We endured staggering misfortunes and severe trials of faith, yet we saw God relentlessly using our experiences to draw lost souls to Christ. After a grand opening service at the beginning of a campaign in the Daytona Beach city auditorium, the building burned almost to the ground, destroying all of the instruments and technical equipment we had collected and maintained so scrupulously down through the years. We held our meeting the following evening in a high school auditorium, singing with nothing but a borrowed guitar, mandolin, and portable organ. We borrowed a large tent from a local man and rows of plush seats from another auditorium and arranged to erect the tent on a baseball field. We held two meetings in the tent before an early morning tropical storm tore the tent to shreds and ruined the plush seats. We moved back into the high school, where the story of our misfortunes doubled the size of our crowds and brought many new converts to Christ! If I could have engineered such disasters for the sake of souls, I would have, but we could only soldier on and see what God would do next!

At one point we were able to purchase a complicated Army Air Corps surplus tent that had been designed as a portable hangar for the B-29 super-bomber. The instructions for putting up this monstrous facility were as thick as a Bible. The hangar's inaugural campaign was set for Bakersfield, California, where the summertime heat was hovering around 110 degrees at midday. As we struggled to erect the tent, my brother-in-law Wayne and I had to wear gloves to keep the metal fixtures from burning our hands. An elderly man watched us work and laughed when he learned we were planning to hold a religious meeting. "There aren't enough Christians in this county to fill two rows of these seats," he advised us. That night the tent was filled to overflowing—for one thing, the B-29 hangar had piqued the public's curiosity—and a state highway patrolman came in complaining that the surrounding roads were blocked.

It was during that tour of California, in the stifling August of 1947, that Maude Aimee presented me with our second son. Don Raymond was born at Los Angeles' Queen of Angels Hospital, a facility destined to become the Dream Center, a tremendous inner-city church and ministry. At three days of age, Don moved into our trailer home (we had traded up to a twenty-five-footer), and a week later he was on the road with us, headed for a revival meeting in Pomona.

Praying for Healing

My father had always prayed, in simple and straightforward fashion, for the sick to be healed. I followed in his footsteps.

But "faith healers" had acquired a bad reputation, and in many cases it was well deserved; and I was uneasy with the theatrics that often accompanied their work: they would lay hands on the sick, and the individual would often fall or even appear to be pushed over. I felt the controversy over this routine unnecessarily overshadowed the value of the ministry. So I took a different tack. I regularly prayed for the sick in our meetings, but always from the stage, while the people in need of prayer stayed in their seats. If God was going to heal them, He could just as easily heal them at that distance as He could with a lot of drama onstage. And He did. Thousands upon thousands have been healed in our meetings over the years. And I thank God for all of this. Still, I always felt more strongly about evangelism than healing, because even a person healed by the Lord today would eventually die, and I cared most of all about that individual's standing before God on that day.

> **If God was going to heal them, He could just as easily heal them at that distance as He could with a lot of drama onstage.**

A longtime member of our church, Daddy Raines, had cancer of the tongue and the throat. He had to be fed intravenously. His son, stationed with the Air Force in Germany, flew home to see him one last time. But we prayed for him. God healed him, and his throat literally grew back. Every Sunday for fifteen years I saw him sitting with his wife in our church services. One day at the end of a service, Daddy Raines shook my hand and let me know they would be absent the following weekend; they were going to Pennsylvania to see relatives. "Have a good trip," I said. They went home and packed their suitcases. Daddy carried them outside, opened the trunk of the car, loaded the suitcases, and fell dead from a heart attack. Instead of going to see his relatives in Pennsylvania, he went to see the Lord in heaven! But his cancer had never returned.

One day my sister Leona and Wayne received word that their son Buddy, a student at Wheaton College, had been severely burned in a campus chemistry lab explosion. Before the doctor would let them see him, he took Wayne aside to explain the extent of his injuries. Buddy's chest had been so damaged by the chemical blast that his heart had stopped beating for several minutes.

"How are his eyes?" Wayne asked anxiously.

The doctor began to sob. "His eyes are destroyed."

Leona and Wayne found their son so disfigured that they hardly recognized him. The only familiar body parts left were his feet. His throat was so burned that he spoke in a croak.

But our whole family went to prayer for Buddy. We prayed simply but fervently. And we prayed persistently, day after day. Within a few weeks, he suddenly seemed to turn a corner; he began to recover rapidly. God was working. God was healing!

Today Buddy's eyesight is perfect. He has not a single scar.

God gave countless healings through our ministry down through the years. In our first church in Ohio, a man named Herb King would become one of the first converts to Christ. We didn't know it at that time, but Herb was unable to stand erect unless he was wearing a steel brace on his spine. Some years before, he had fallen into a cooling vat during his work at an Ohio Edison plant. His spine had been broken in several places. A week or so after he came to Christ, Herb came to me after our Sunday service and asked for prayer to help his physical ailment. Since I didn't know what his ailment was, I said a simple prayer. When I finished, he said to me with a smile, "Where can I go to take this thing off?"

"Take what thing off?" I asked.

"This steel brace I'm wearing on my back," he replied.

Wayne led Herb to the basement. There, Herb removed his jacket, then his shirt, and finally the brace. He proceeded to bend over and touch his toes without feeling any pain.

"I'm cured!" he announced.

80

For years we saw him every Sunday at church, and he never wore a brace again!

A Mortgage on a Tent

After Rex Jr.'s miraculous recovery from tuberculosis, we traveled so constantly in ministry that he attended eleven different schools during his first year as a student! He also learned to play Gospel tunes with cowbells and sleigh bells and became a popular performer in our musical group.

By that time, our ministry was, in a way, *too* successful. We had long since given up hope of planning indoor revival meetings in civic or private auditoriums. The facilities were simply too small for our crowds. In the late 1940s, we had contacted hundreds of auditoriums all over the country and found fewer than ten available. We faced the fact that we would have to use a tent. After our struggles with the surplus B-29 hangar in California, we were inclined to look for something more efficient. By God's grace we were able to buy a secondhand tent that Oral Roberts was discarding.

Traveling with a tent was always an ordeal. Heavy rainstorms and lashing winds would rip our patched-up canvas. We would pull it down, sew it up, then put it up again before the evening service, doing all the work in the pouring rain. And when cold weather came, of course, a tent was uncomfortable.

One spring day in South Bend, Indiana, as I surveyed the lot where we planned to pitch our tent, I met an advance man for the Ringling Brothers and Barnum & Bailey Circus; he was selecting a site nearby for his show's big top. We compared our duties.

"My job," he said, "is to check the lot for our tent, order hay to scatter around the grounds in case it gets muddy, and make arrangements for our crew to put up the tent when our show arrives. We have three other men who came here last week to handle advertising and other advance arrangements. What do you do for your show?"

"Well, let's see," I replied. "I rent the lot, get permits from city hall, make arrangements for electricity, transportation, radio broadcasts, and telephone lines if we're picking up radio programs from our tent. I solicit help and cooperation from local churches, and arrange to use their members at our services as ushers and as counselors for guiding our converts. When the tent arrives, I help drive in the stakes, stretch the canvas, and build the platform where my father preaches and our Humbard Family group sings. I see to the sound equipment and amplifiers. Then when our show opens, I'm in the pulpit, greeting the people and acting as the master of ceremonies."

The circus man's eyes were big.

"One guy can't do all that," he said.

"I guess I'm kind of like a bumblebee," I answered. "The scientist examines the structure of a bumblebee, weighs it, and says that according to the laws of aeronautics, the bee shouldn't be able to fly. But the bee doesn't know that, so he just goes ahead and flies anyway, because God wants him to fly, rules or no rules."

"You know something?" the circus man said. "Maybe you're the ones who have the greatest show on earth."

The circus arrived in South Bend a few days after we opened our meeting. I got up at 4:00 a.m., as I had in my boyhood in Hot Springs, to watch them put up their tent. It seemed gigantic compared to our secondhand shelter.

"God's work shouldn't be second best to anything," I said to myself. "We ought to get ourselves the biggest and the finest tent that money can buy."

The patched-up tent we had bought from Oral Roberts seated 3,000 people. I wanted one twice that big and more efficient and easier to put up and take down. I drove from South Bend to Chicago and talked to one of the biggest tent-manufacturing companies. They figured that a 6,000-seat big top like the one I described would cost $21,000. They would start work when I gave them a down payment of $6,000. The tent would be delivered to us when we paid the balance of $15,000. I knew we could never take on such a huge debt unless God wanted us to have such a tent. I went back to South Bend to pray about it.

We decided to "put out a fleece to God" as Gideon did in the Old Testament. I told the Lord that if we received $1,000 in our Sunday evening collection, an unusually generous total, I would take it as a sign that God wanted us to go ahead and get the new, larger tent.

On the following Sunday evening, I explained to the people our need for a bigger tent. I told them I had put out a fleece to God to get His answer to our question. I did not plead for an unusually large collection, nor did I reveal the specific sum I had prayed for. I asked the people to put into the offering only what God prompted them to give. When the offering was counted that night, it added up to $1,060. We ordered the tent. Within the next few weeks, our generous friends in South Bend raised the $6,000 we needed for the down payment.

After the close of our South Bend meetings, we needed to spend a few weeks with the tent makers in Chicago, going over the details of the structural plans. So we decided to hold a revival in the Windy City. We were warned that Chicago was no place for evangelism, that people there were notoriously cold toward our kind of old-fashioned, country-style preaching. But our meetings there were packed every night, and people flocked to the platform each evening answering the call to accept Christ. We were amazed to meet many senior citizens who said that they had never prayed before.

As we worked with the tent makers on our plans for the new big top, I was struck by another brainstorm. We were tired of building a platform for a stage every time we erected our tent, and then tearing it down as we planned to move to the next stop. I visualized a big trailer truck with sides that could be folded down to form a platform, with built-in electrical wiring for lighting and sound equipment. I made arrangements with a trailer company in Chicago to design such a stage on wheels, which could be driven inside our new tent and made ready for services within a few minutes. On the road, the same trailer could carry all of our sound and musical equipment, which now included an organ, a piano, a harp, a vibraphone, cowbells and sleigh bells, a bass fiddle, guitars, and accordions. In our Chicago meetings, where we were warned we would fail, our offerings were so large that they covered the down payment on this magnificent trailer and the tractor to pull it.

Of course, there was still the matter of paying off the tent. During the next few months, while we held a series of seventeen-day meetings in Indiana and Arkansas, I visited banks in every city of both states, trying to borrow the remaining $15,000. Banks weren't interested in taking a mortgage on a tent, I was told again and again. What would a bank want with a tent, if we fell behind in our payments and the tent had to be repossessed?

I was getting nowhere when an invitation came from old friends in Oakland to hold a month of revival meetings in their church. I hesitated. It was January of 1950, and it seemed like a long, cold, difficult trip for a single month of ministry. But I prayed about it, and God told us to go to Oakland.

I soon discovered why. In a local bank, cashing a check, I met a teller who seemed particularly friendly, and on a sudden impulse I asked him for the name of the bank's loan department manager. The teller directed me to the proper desk. There, I told the manager I wanted to borrow $15,000 for a mortgage and insurance on a tent. The manager picked up a telephone, called an insurance broker, and asked, "Would you insure a tent?" There was a brief pause. "Yes, that's what I said—a tent."

When he hung up, he told me that the broker would be coming by in a few minutes to work out the details.

It seemed unbelievable. This bank was willing to take a mortgage at lower interest than I expected to pay, and the insurance premium was about half the rate quoted to me by companies in Chicago and Little Rock. In a slight daze, I signed the papers. The check for $15,000 was sent to the tent-manufacturing company the next day. While I had been criss-crossing the Midwest in search of financing, God had the whole transaction already arranged for me half a country away!

Our new Gospel Big Top made its grand debut a few weeks later in Houston, hailed by headlines and attracting huge crowds. There was a lump in my throat as I watched that vast canvas go up and stretch into shape for the first time. I thought of the thirteen-year-old boy who watched the crowd pouring into the circus tent in Hot Springs twenty years earlier, saying to himself, "If only God had a tent like that, He'd have a crowd like that!" Now God finally had a tent as big as the Ringling Brothers big top. And the Gospel Big Top would give people more than temporary entertainment; here they would receive the key to eternal salvation.

A Hunch About Baltimore

We ministered in Alabama, Texas, Oklahoma, Kansas, Missouri, a continuous series of revival meetings under the Gospel Big Top. Rex Jr. had been switching schools every seventeen days for so long that Maude Aimee finally took our sons to Hot Springs for the school year; she worked at the Gospel Temple with my sister Ruth and her husband, Louis Davidson, the pastor. We were reunited for the summer, then packed our trucks and headed to Canton, Ohio, where a friend had invited us to conduct a revival.

In Canton, two reporters from the Akron *Beacon Journal* were planning a story on a famous jazz band appearing at Meyers Lake Park, but on the way they saw our huge tent and crowds streaming into it. They stopped to see what was going on, stayed for our service, and wrote their feature about our ministry instead of the jazz band! From the day the article appeared, hundreds of people drove the twenty-five miles from Akron to Canton to attend our services each evening. (And, as it turned out, this was the beginning of a long and complicated relationship with the *Beacon Journal.*)

We were scheduled to move on to Baltimore, where local churches had offered us enthusiastic sponsorship and cooperation. A few days before the end of our stay in Canton, I flew to Baltimore to check the arrangements there. I found that the city authorities were donating to us, free of charge, an excellent location for our tent, inside a public park near a main highway. Everybody in Baltimore was friendly, and all of them told me how much they were looking forward to our visit.

But something was wrong.

Something inside me said, Don't go.

I pay attention to such impressions—what my father always called "hunches"—because so often I find that God is the One speaking. A few years earlier we were in Owensboro, Kentucky, and I went to Covington to check arrangements for the upcoming meeting we had scheduled there. Everything seemed fine: the tent site was good, radio arrangements were exceptional, and local churches and city officials offered all the help we needed. Furthermore, our Owensboro meeting had been disappointing, so I should have been glad to move on to Covington. But God spoke to my spirit silently and prompted me to stay in Owensboro another week. Three days later, Covington was devastated by a tornado.

I had no such feeling of impending doom in Baltimore, only a strong urge to go elsewhere. I took a plane back to Ohio, where Wayne was waiting for me at Akron–Canton Airport.

"We're not going to Baltimore," I said.

"I thought we were all set there!" he replied.

"We are all set there," I said. "But I just don't feel right about going to Baltimore, and I don't know why."

Then, on an impulse, I asked Wayne for a favor: "How about driving me to Akron?"

In the back of my mind was that favorable article appearing in the *Beacon Journal*, and the large groups of people coming to our Canton meetings from Akron. As we drove north we approached the Rubber Bowl, Akron's big stadium, and Derby Downs, home of the soapbox derby.

"Wouldn't it be terrific if we could set up our tent near Derby Downs?" I said to Wayne. "What a place for a meeting!"

"Derby Downs?" Wayne echoed, dubiously. There was silence for a moment. "Well," he finally added, "maybe you're right."

Little did we know that we would be staying in Akron for more than three decades.

GOD'S CRAZINESS

I soon found out, to my astonishment, that Akron was perhaps the only city in America where a tent cannot be erected for a public gathering without a special vote of the city council.

So there I was, turning down a warm invitation from the city government in Baltimore, going instead to a place where we would have to wait out several days of legal wrangling before we would even know if we could pitch our tent. As my family made painfully clear to me, it didn't seem to make much sense.

But God was still telling me to go to Akron. On a Friday, two days before we were to close our Canton meeting, the legal department at Akron city hall helped me draw up special paperwork for a tent permit. On Monday our Gospel Big Top had been taken down and packed onto our trucks in Canton, where my family was waiting to find out where to head next. I was telephoning the newspaper in Baltimore, telling them not to publish the advertisements of our coming meeting there until they heard from me. Finally, at 4:00 p.m. on Tuesday, the city council in Akron voted to let us set up our tent at the Municipal Airport grounds, near Derby Downs. I called Wayne in Canton and asked him to get our trucks rolling into Akron; we would open a meeting within days. Then I called the papers in Baltimore and, finally, the church people there who were expecting us. It was embarrassing, but I had to tell them we had decided to call off our meeting there.

The schedule was crazy, and yet it was God's craziness. We were so rushed in setting up our unscheduled visit to Akron that I had no time to solicit sponsorship and support from the established churches there, as I normally did before opening a revival in a new location. God engineered this departure from the norm. If I had come to Akron under the sponsorship of any of the local pastors, I would never have felt free to stay there and establish an independent church.

And that is exactly what God had in mind.

Impossible in the Natural

During our stay in Canton, many area residents had asked us to invite Kathryn Kuhlman, the dynamic evangelist from Pittsburgh, to be a guest speaker at one of our meetings. I had never met Kathryn, so I went to Pittsburgh to hear her preach. She made a powerful impression on me, not so much by her eloquence or her prayers for healing the sick, but by the huge numbers of people who answered her altar calls. I invited her to speak at our first Sunday service in Akron, and she was glad to accept. She had wanted to appear in Akron but hadn't been able to find an auditorium large enough.

We announced that Kathryn Kuhlman would appear at our tent for services at 11:00 a.m. that Sunday. At 4:00 a.m., a policeman knocked on the door of our trailer home. He had interesting news. All 6,000 seats of our tent were already filled, and several thousand more people were standing outside. We learned later that more than 1,500 of the people attending our Saturday service the night before had simply remained in their seats all night to be sure of a place inside the tent when Kathryn Kuhlman arrived!

Police and newspaper reporters estimated that the crowds gathered at our tent that day (inside and outside) totaled more than 18,000. The Gospel Big Top had its side walls rolled up, and the people stood in great circles stretching all the way around the tent—twenty-five circles deep. We began a series of back-to-back services at 7:30 that morning, continuing nonstop until after 1:30 in the afternoon. More than 1,150 people answered Kathryn's altar calls, and no doubt there were many more converts unable to make their way forward through the crush of the crowd.

Twenty-one years later, when Kathryn Kuhlman appeared at our Cathedral of Tomorrow for the celebration of my fortieth year in ministry, the scene repeated itself. Before midnight on Saturday, people were lined up outside the closed doors of the church, and parking lots for miles around were jammed. We opened the doors at 7:30 Sunday morning. Within thirty minutes, the Cathedral's seats were filled; all available standing room was filled; some of the aisles were filled: a total of more than 7,000 people were present. Thousands were turned away, since unfortunately we couldn't roll up the side walls of the Cathedral! Kathryn started preaching at 9:00 a.m., nearly two hours ahead of schedule, and continued until almost 1:00 p.m. That night, Johnny Cash was scheduled to appear. Running five separate cameras, we finished the day with more than twenty miles of videotape!

The overflow crowds attracted to Kathryn Kuhlman's first appearance in our tent, back in 1952, stirred up a storm of excitement and made headlines for weeks. Sadly, the pastor of one of the largest local churches, Dallas Billington, who had invited our family to appear at his church some years before, now attacked us in print because of our association with Kathryn Kuhlman. Billington was opposed to Kathryn's Pentecostal faith in the healing power of God's Holy Spirit, and he was clearly upset by the popular success of her appearance in our tent. The newspaper, loving a good controversy for the sake of selling papers, quoted him as vowing "to run the Humbards out of town." But my father and I both refused to enter the controversy, and the publicity only increased the size of the crowds at our nightly meetings and those at Kathryn's return appearances on the next three Sunday mornings.

A friend later asked me how much of a donation we had made to Billington's church, because the fuss he stirred up drew more attention to our Gospel Big Top revival services than any advertising we could have afforded!

The only problem with all that publicity was our lack of facilities and personnel; we weren't prepared to handle such enormous crowds, the biggest throngs we had ever seen in all our years as traveling evangelists. Families in the surrounding neighborhoods were complaining to city authorities, and who could blame them? There was noise; there was confusion; there was traffic congestion every evening. There was the commotion of parking cars on their neighborhood streets. Charles Slussor, Akron's mayor, finally came to us, full of regrets, and told us he would have to revoke our permit. We would have to move out of the city.

But then came Clare Conlan. He was a prominent local citizen who had come to Christ in one of our meetings a few days earlier, and he pleaded our case to the mayor and city council. They agreed to let us move our tent to another location on the airport grounds, where we could use the parking lots and sanitary facilities of the Rubber Bowl without disturbing the nearby residential neighborhoods.

We were given this permission on a Friday and were told that we could wait till Monday before beginning the three-day process of dismantling our tent and setting it up again on the other side of the airport. But this would evaporate our weekend ministry schedule, so I went to prayer. I asked God to help us move the tent Friday night and complete the setup before our Saturday evening service. It was impossible in the natural, but of course God was unfazed. I made an appeal on our radio broadcast that afternoon and in our Gospel Big Top service that evening for volunteer workers. We heard that wives were telephoning their husbands at the Goodyear and Firestone rubber plants and asking them to stop off at the airport on their way home from work to help us with the gargantuan project. Hundreds of men and women showed up to work with us throughout the night.

The vast roof of our huge tent was supported by steel columns fifty-five feet high. Instead of dismantling them, which would have taken too much time and work, our volunteers clustered around each pole, lifting them simultaneously and walking them across the airport grounds—carrying the entire upper structure of the tent above their heads. It was one of the most amazing displays of strength and careful teamwork I have ever seen.

By the following afternoon, we had the Gospel Big Top erected in its new location, with electrical fixtures connected and the seats, platform, and sound equipment in place. On Saturday evening, we held our usual baptism service!

HOME BASE

Our crowds in Akron were so huge at every meeting that we decided to extend our originally scheduled seventeen-day stay to five weeks. Even on closing night, every seat was taken and hundreds more were standing in the aisles, listening to or singing along with our Gospel songs and listening to Dad's Bible message. During those five weeks in Akron, our services were attended by more than 200,000 people—certainly a record for such an outdoor religious revival meeting and all the more remarkable in light of the fact that the population of Akron itself was only 275,000 at the time.

We finally moved our Gospel Big Top to Cleveland, thirty miles to the north, where the tent was again filled to overflowing every night. Maude Aimee and I began to see the same faces in our Cleveland audiences that we had come to recognize in Akron; people were driving sixty miles round trip to experience our ministry in Cleveland!

I began to think seriously about Akron. We already had a warm feeling about the people. The huge crowds there and in Canton and Cleveland convinced me that the people of northeast Ohio, one of the most densely populated areas in the United States, were particularly receptive to our style of evangelism. It occurred to me to concentrate our future work there, instead of making long tours to far-flung corners of the country, as we had for the past decade. My family wanted to pack up the tent and hold winter meetings in Florida or California; I talked them into spending the winter in Akron, putting the tent into storage. My idea was to establish a home base in Akron, where our families could live and send our growing children to school. We could rent the Copley Theater for the winter, stage nightly meetings, produce daily morning and evening radio broadcasts on WAKR, and build up a following during the winter. Then, in the other nine months of the year, while still keeping our homes in Akron, we could hold a series of ten-day outdoor tent meetings in nearby cities: Youngstown, Pittsburgh, Cleveland, Toledo, Fort Wayne, Indianapolis, Canton, and Columbus, as well as a return engagement at Derby Downs.

We began according to plan: we rented the Copley Theater, which held almost a thousand people, and began nightly meetings, which were completely packed every evening. Our daily radio programs, mornings and evenings on an Akron station, were so successful that we were soon being beamed to stations in Cleveland, Pittsburgh, and Wheeling, West Virginia.

But after just a month, my father was fidgety. He wanted to take the tent out of storage. He wanted to move to a warmer part of the country. A year-round ministry in the Akron area didn't interest him.

I found myself talking with Maude Aimee and Wayne and Leona about establishing a church in Akron, but not just a church. It would be a church seen on nationwide television! It was, on the face of it, unthinkable. No such thing had ever existed!

FIVE

A Vision of the Future

$\mathcal{W}$e had been on television only rarely. During a crusade in Oklahoma City, a Nazarene pastor with a small TV program invited me to appear on the air and promote our meetings. During a Gospel Big Top campaign in Houston, we had arranged to do a television program. I was impressed with the impact, but God had much more in store.

One day I was in downtown Akron getting a haircut in the barber shop of the Mayflower Hotel. As I walked out, I saw a crowd gathered on the sidewalk across the street in front of the O'Neill department store. I thought someone had been hurt; I headed across to see if I could help.

But there was no injury. There was just a glass display window, and behind it was a tiny television set. A speaker had been rigged to the outdoors. On the screen was a grainy, flickering black-and-white image: the Cleveland Indians were playing the New York Yankees.

Cleveland got a hit, and the crowd erupted with cheers. A Cleveland player stole a base, and the people exploded again.

"This is powerful," I said to myself. "God ought to be on television!"

Akron did not even have a television station; the TV set in the window was tuned to a Cleveland station. But somehow, God planted in my heart, in that moment, a vision of the future.

* * *

The great crowds that came to our outdoor meetings that fall had convinced me that more and more people were hungry for God. Jesus had clearly stated in Matthew 24:14 that "this gospel of the kingdom shall be preached in all the world for a witness unto all nations; and then shall the end come" (KJV). And it was clear to me, with the world's population mushrooming, that even a Gospel Big Top, seating six thousand, was not up to the challenge. The only medium of communication capable of spreading the Gospel to all the world in our lifetime was TV.

I had no hunger to be a TV star; I was hungry to reach people. I didn't want to preach the Gospel from a television studio or from public auditoriums or outdoor sports stadiums. I wanted to bring into the homes of people who weren't attending church the sights and sounds of Sunday services in an interdenominational church filled with soul-searching and God-seeking men and women. I wanted people at home to get into the habit of participating every Sunday in churches in their living rooms, watching and listening to a congregation praying, singing, listening to Gospel music and Bible preaching, and seeing people coming forward to the altar to profess their newfound faith in Jesus Christ. I wanted viewers to begin attending church services in their own hometowns. I wanted to use television to lead them to trust Christ. In those days, it was a radical idea, although today it's almost unimaginable against the wall-to-wall backdrop of televised church services.

And the first step would be to establish a church. Akron was clearly the place to do that; the people of the city had been unusually kind and warmly responsive. I had made many close friends during our Gospel Big Top campaign.

But as I talked with my family, it was clear that my father and brother didn't get it. Dad still wanted to head to Florida for the winter. Clement wanted to do a tour in California.

Maude Aimee was simply committed to doing God's will. "Whatever you feel God wants you to do will be all right with me," she said. Wayne and Leona were willing to stay with us too; Wayne promised to be "the best assistant pastor any pastor ever had."

My parents finally left snowy Akron and headed back to Hot Springs for Christmas. My brother and his wife left on vacation. We all agreed that Dad and Clement would return to Akron at the end of January and take our tent, trucks, and traveling equipment out of storage, going back on the road for a series of meetings in a warmer part of the country. Maude Aimee and I would decide before then whether to head out with them or to stay behind in Akron and start a church. I asked God to help me make a firm decision on Christmas Day.

True to their word, Wayne and Leona stayed with us when the others left. To earn a few much-needed dollars, Wayne had gotten himself a job in Cleveland with a company manufacturing gymnasium equipment, but he worked with us faithfully every night and every weekend at the Copley Theater. With my father gone, I had to learn fast how to be a preacher. For the first time in my life, I was delivering the message every night and again on our radio program every day. I was hardly prepared to pastor a church. I had done many other jobs in my family's ministry but not much preaching. And now on top of everything else, I felt guilty at the prospect of leaving them to fend for themselves in all the areas I had covered.

I tried to talk God out of this whole insane idea.

"Lord, I don't know how to be a pastor," I prayed. "I don't know much about preaching. Let me stay at the work I'm doing, managing the road tours for my folks. Maybe this whole idea of a church with a television audience is just a crazy notion that will never work out."

Meanwhile, Maude Aimee and I were facing another problem that threatened to keep us from staying in Akron that winter: we couldn't find a heated apartment or house for rent. And with two small boys, we couldn't spend the winter in our house trailer. Just when it appeared that we would have to close down our nightly services at the Copley and move to a warmer climate simply for lack of lodging, the phone rang. A woman had heard that one of her neighbors would be spending the next three months in Florida, and would we like to rent the house? Yes!

The week before Christmas was hard. Wayne and Leona had been invited to spend the holiday with Wayne's employer in Florida; we urged them to accept the invitation because they were long overdue for a vacation. But this left Maude Aimee and me alone, carrying on the work, conducting services at the theater every evening, producing two radio programs every day, and parenting Rex Jr. and Don! Somehow, with Maude Aimee on vocals and me on guitar and sermons, we managed.

"Go for It, Kids!"

Maude Aimee and I had grown close to Kathryn Kuhlman, and now we wanted her advice. We arranged to visit her at her home in Pittsburgh, and I laid out the entire dream for her: Television ought to be used for God, and since nobody was doing it, I wanted to put a church service on television. Kathryn listened intently. When I was finished, she asked me to tell it to her all over again. I did, explaining that I had managed the family ministry for twenty years, but my family didn't want to stay, and I could hardly sleep because of this vision God had planted in my heart.

Finally Kathryn leaned close to me.

"Are you sure this is what God wants you to do?" she asked.

"Kathryn, I'm sure," I replied.

She doubled up her fist and shook it at us.

"Go for it, kids!" she shouted.

Kathryn became one of our most committed supporters. Down through the years, she was probably Maude Aimee's dearest friend. She sometimes invited Maude Aimee to take "a few days' rest." They would go to New York City just to shop or to sit in the lobby of the Plaza Hotel and watch celebrities come in and out! Kathryn ministered with us many times over the years, always asking Maude Aimee to sing her favorite song, "We'll Talk It Over in the By and By." Her death, in 1976, hit us hard.

* * *

I got little sleep on Christmas Eve. I wrestled with the decision I had committed myself to make the next day. When I got out of bed on Christmas morning, I prayed that God would give me His answer by leading me to it in the pages of the Bible. I opened my Bible at random and saw the words of Matthew 8:26: "Why are ye fearful, O ye of little faith? Then he arose, and rebuked the winds and the sea; and there was a great calm" (KJV).

A great calm came over my heart, too. I had found the answer; my doubts and hesitation vanished. I would stay. We would build a strong church. We would devote ourselves to bringing God's Word to people all over the world.

My parents and my brother had also locked in on their decisions. My parents wanted to return to pastoring the church in Hot Springs. My brother Clem wanted to take the tent and continue the traveling evangelism ministry. I handed over the tent, the trucks, and trailers, and the equipment.

On a cold February morning in 1953, I watched our family's vehicles pull out of Akron, loaded with our Gospel Big Top. I waved good-bye and tried to swallow the lump of sadness in my throat. There I was, on my own in ministry for the first time in my life, with nothing but a car, a small trailer home, and sixty-five dollars cash.

The nearness of God, the love of my wife, and the loyalty of Wayne and Leona were huge for me that day. Maude Aimee was sharing my dream. Wayne and Leona were making a big personal sacrifice; his boss had offered him three times more than he could ever receive through our church if he would join the company full time.

We also had many faithful friends in Akron pulling for us. Clare Conlan, who had pulled strings with the city council to get our tent up, was a prominent real estate dealer and a former potentate of the local Shriners, and he, too, was in our corner. We would need God, family, and every friend we had to make it through the next few months.

BLINDERS ON

Dallas Billington decided to become a major adversary. We were not his first target, however. Well before I came to town, Billington had taken up a campaign against the United Way because, in his view, they supported Catholic organizations but not Protestant ones. There were members of Billington's church working in the various major tire companies of Akron, and he distributed leaflets throughout the companies urging a boycott of the United Way. He also used his local radio program to rail against the United Way. It was a painfully effective campaign; so much so that the United Way arranged for the Akron *Beacon Journal* to negotiate a backroom settlement with Billington. If he would end the boycott, the United Way would start supporting some Protestant charities, and the newspaper would give him favorable coverage.

With such a deal in place, it followed that the *Beacon Journal* would give big play to Billington's rants when Kathryn Kuhlman came to town. And they were equally supportive of him as he continued his attacks on me in the years that followed. "That Rex Humbard," he would say on the radio. "You go out there and he'll rub a greasy palm all over your forehead, and he'll have his other hand in your back pocket. One of these days he'll leave town and he'll have all your money."

I was astonished by his anger, but not too rattled. My response strategy was quite simple. I would go into my little office in our house on Grant Street, close and lock the door behind me, get down on my knees, and pray for Dallas Billington and for his congregation. It was not easy— I made myself do it—but it was effective. I walked out of that house, down the street toward our church; I could feel the electricity of God's love. I could feel His divine anointing. I was free; I had nothing in my heart against anyone. Billington could blast me on his 6:15 p.m. radio show, but I could preach the Word of God at 7:30, and people would come to Christ; the sick would be healed. I never spent a moment broadcasting criticism of Dallas Billington or the Akron *Beacon Journal* or any of our other detractors; I spent all my time and energy in search of lost souls; and God fought the battles!

Decades later, when I revealed this story, my son Rex Jr. said to me, "I never understood why you would allow that jerk across town to slap you around like he did. I never knew that you got down on your knees and asked God to bless Dallas Billington and his congregation. Now what we lived through makes sense to me!"

When I was young, we used a horse-drawn plow. Before heading through a cornfield, we put blinders on the horse. Without the blinders, the horse would see the corn and eat it himself. But with the blinders, the animal was able to stay on his assigned task and accomplish the job. I have advised many ministers to take the same approach. Put blinders on.

Ignore criticism. What's your goal? Stay in line and head there. Your ministry doesn't depend on people's opinion of you. It depends on God's opinion of you; the condition of your heart is the crucial component.

Sometimes it seems that criticism is called for. In my youth I was horrified to learn of a minister, whom I can only describe as a rascal, renting Cadle Tabernacle in Indianapolis, announcing a revival, and packing out the facility. He was a brilliant preacher; he had conducted revivals all across America that shook whole cities for Christ. Yet he had left his wife and taken up with a girlfriend; his lifestyle was scandalous and his ministry tactics were outrageous. He put barrels at the front of the auditorium and told people to throw in their "worldly" apparel, everything from wedding rings to shorts, and get rid of them. At the end of his extremely emotional sermon, people would come to Christ, and he would walk out the back door, get into a limousine with his girlfriend, and head to their room in a local hotel. My spirit was shredded by the hypocrisy. But eventually God led me to 1 Corinthians 13: "Though I speak with the tongues of men and of angels,…understand all mysteries and all knowledge,…bestow all my goods to feed the poor, and…my body to be burned but have not love"—divine love in my heart—"it profits me nothing" (verses 1-3). In those words, I saw the rascal. He could stand up there and give an altar call, and people could actually get saved, because God would honor the sinner's prayer, but there would be no ultimate spiritual benefit to the rascal himself. God could continue to use him "for the gifts and the calling of God are irrevocable," Romans 11:29 says, but it would "profit him nothing," because he didn't have the love of God in his own heart. The day came when I

> He could stand up there and give an altar call, and people could actually get saved, because God would honor the sinner's prayer.

relaxed; I quit worrying about rascals like him. "Lord, they're your problem," I prayed.

A Thousand Times Too Much

Our lease on the Copley Theater was soon to run out; Akron's new television station WAKR was taking it over as a TV studio. As we prayed and searched for a new location for the church we were planning, I hired a small plane and flew over the city to see how and where it was growing. From the air, the most attractive and promising part of the Akron area was on the other side of the high level bridge, in Cuyahoga Falls, the suburb just north of Akron. A vacant movie house, the Ohio Theater on State Road, was ideal; but it was for sale, not for rent, and the price was $140,000. That was a fair figure in 1953; but the owners wanted $65,000 down, about a thousand times as much as I had!

Clare Conlan came to the rescue again, calling a meeting of our friends in Akron to see how much money we might scrape together. Their pledges of support were so encouraging that I went to talk with the owners of the Ohio Theater, not once or twice, but several times. At each meeting, they lowered the size of the down payment, but it was still miles higher than we could afford to pay.

Then Maude Aimee visited the Ohio Theater for the first time. She was dazzled by the possibilities. Her sharp artistic eye took in various features of the auditorium that could be remodeled or redecorated to our advantage. She pressed her hand against a wall of the theater, closed her eyes, and prayed, "God, if this is the building You've picked out for us, help us to get it!"

Maude Aimee's enthusiasm sent me back to the books. I rechecked our pledges. I refigured our risks. I made several overoptimistic calculations. Then I went back to the owners of the theater with a proposition that seemed, to all my friends, completely preposterous, even embarrassing. I offered no large down payment, only $5,000 on signing and another $5,000 on possession; the rest of the $140,000 would come in monthly payments of $5,000 over the next two years.

There was no way they would accept such a schedule—but they did. Not only did they say yes immediately, but when they learned how much expensive remodeling would have to be done to change the theater into a church, they offered to cut the monthly payments from $5,000 to $2,000! I still didn't know where we were going to get that much money, but I knew God was on our side.

We would never miss a payment.

TRANSFORMATION

We had to work fast. The building was turned over to us in early March; we had to be out of the Copley Theater by April 1. We aimed for a grand opening of our new church home on Easter Sunday, April 5, 1953, less than a month away.

Many of our friends pitched in to help us with carpentry, painting, electrical wiring; many worked deep into the night after working at their own jobs during the day. But I still found the going rough: while I was working with plumbers, carpenters, and painters all day long, I was still preaching every night at our Copley Theater services, and still producing three radio programs, one of which was an hour-long Christian disc-jockey show with Gospel music recordings and talks on spiritual and family problems. And it was live, from 12:30 to 1:30 in the morning!

Finally my friend Clare Conlan caught me trying to work on a sermon while fielding questions from workmen about lumber for the new platform. He suggested letting him send me to Florida for the five days before Easter, to hole up in his trailer in St. Petersburg, meditate and pray, and prepare my Easter Sunday message. Maude Aimee insisted I take the offer. "The nicest church in the world won't mean much," she said, "unless you have something worthwhile prepared to serve to the folks after they come in here." And she refused to leave the work behind to join me. "Go on down there to Florida where it's peaceful," she said, "and have a heart-to-heart talk with the Lord."

Five days before our grand opening, we closed our final meeting at the Copley Theater, and Maude Aimee drove me to the Cleveland airport. When she picked me up at the same place on Saturday, I wanted her to drive me directly to Calvary Temple so I could see how the auditorium looked.

"No, Rex," she replied. "I'm taking you home, and you'll wait there until 10:30. We were up all last night getting things finished, and I promised the folks I wouldn't let you see the church until it's completely done."

I learned later that Maude Aimee and the volunteers had actually been working straight through for three days and two nights. I was feeling fine, completely Florida rested, but Maude Aimee was more exhausted than I had ever seen her.

When I finally walked into the new Calvary Temple auditorium, I couldn't speak. The transformation was thrilling. I walked down the aisle with tears in my eyes. A new pulpit stood on the stage. Maude Aimee gave me a new Bible with a bright red cover, something I had never seen.

"The red cover signifies the blood of Jesus Christ that was shed for us," she told me. "I didn't want to give you an old-fashioned black-covered Bible, because I don't want you to look like an old-fashioned pastor. I want you to be a new and up-to-date kind of a pastor."

I carried that red Bible to church every Sunday morning for decades. It still holds a place of honor in my study.

Easter Sunday morning dawned gray and rainy, typical of an Akron spring. We had asked God to send 1,000 children for our new Sunday school; despite the rain, 1,027 youngsters enrolled. Maude Aimee was exhausted and suffered from a throat infection; her voice was reduced to a muffled croak. She warned me she wouldn't be able to sing. But as I walked onto the platform before our overflowing congregation to open the first Easter service in our first "church of our own," I had to call on Maude Aimee for a solo. She shook her head; she knew it was impossible. So I asked the congregation to pray for her. I placed my hand on her and asked the Lord to heal her throat so she could sing for His glory. God answered my prayer immediately. Maude Aimee came to the microphone and her clear, bell-like tones soared through the auditorium as she sang my favorite of all the old Gospel songs, "We'll Talk It Over."

We had another service in the afternoon, with another crowd almost as large. At seven in the evening the auditorium was so crowded that folding chairs were placed in every available extra space, and still there were hundreds of people standing.

I spoke to our people from a full heart, thanking God for their support in establishing this new church. I asked Maude Aimee to come forward and join me in expressing our thanks, but she was too deeply moved to speak. Trying to ease her strain, I joked, "Well, honey, at least tell these folks that you're glad you married me."

Then she spoke.

"Friends, I'm glad I married Rex," she said. "We've had a wonderful marriage. Some of it has been hard, but we've always been happy. The Lord has been so good to us. I only hope God will continue to keep Rex as humble and thankful for God's blessings as he was this morning when he walked down this aisle with tears streaming down his face."

And I could only agree.

SIX

The Thirteenth Visit

So the Ohio Theater became the interdenominational Calvary Temple. Outside we erected a red and green neon-lighted forty-two-foot cross so people passing by would take notice that the previous entertainment center was now a soul-saving station.

Calvary Temple had more than a thousand seats, but the crowds at our Sunday services were always too big for the church to hold, even when we conducted five services on a Sunday. Our Sunday school attendance was soon so high that we had to rent two nearby public schools for classroom space. Our adult Bible class, with Wayne as teacher, filled the entire auditorium of the church. Every Sunday, we rented twenty-two city buses to transport members who had no other means of getting to and from church. Our buses stopped at regular city bus stops; anybody waiting could get on and ride free of charge. We soon found that Catholics were riding our buses to the Catholic churches, which was perfectly fine with me. As long as they were going to church, I didn't care which church they attended!

Our church soon became busy with various activities—prayer groups, youth programs, mission-supporting services, spiritual counseling, and visitation work—not only on Sundays but every day and evening of the week. We organized an enthusiastic choir and an eighteen-piece orchestra. We had three daily radio programs on local stations, a twenty-four-hour dial-a-prayer service, and a monthly devotional magazine. All this sudden growth of warm Christian fellowship in our new and devoted congregation strengthened my conviction about people's spiritual hunger. It seemed clear that the world was hungry to worship Jesus Christ without regard for any dividing doctrines of sect or denomination.

So the paint was hardly dry on Calvary Temple when I started on the next step in our plan: trying to put our church services on television. A few months after we opened Calvary Temple, we were doing a half-hour program on Saturday afternoons on a Cleveland TV station. Then, when WAKR opened Akron's first full-fledged television station, our Sunday services were broadcast live. This was our first real step forward—weekly live broadcasts of our church services—but it was only local television.

To get statewide coverage, I aimed at WXEL, the Storer Broadcasting Company TV station in Cleveland (which would later become WJW, and finally WJKW). But the Storer company, like the big television networks and other chains of stations, had a strict policy of barring religious programs for fear of offending advertising sponsors and viewers who might not share certain religious beliefs. Only the independent stations were willing to sell TV time to evangelists. Still, I was determined, with the help of God, to put our Sunday church services on that Storer station in Cleveland, the major city closest to Akron and the obvious first choice for beginning our "network expansion."

I had managed to get my foot in the door at WXEL by arranging to buy time on the channel for a Saturday Gospel music program featuring Maude Aimee, Wayne and Leona, and other musicians from our Calvary

Temple singing group. The station's management reminded me of its policy against religious programs and sternly warned me against doing any Bible preaching on our show. For the first few months, I was careful not to do any talking between songs. Eventually I gently asked the station manager if I could say a few words to the audience now and then, assuring him I wouldn't do any strong Bible preaching, just "inspirational talks." Reluctantly, he agreed.

When the letters and phone calls began coming in, viewers praising the inspirational messages, the management asked me to *keep on talking!*

Soon I was paying weekly visits to the Storer station's office, urging the manager to pick up our church services live from Akron and transmit them from his station in Cleveland as a weekly Sunday morning feature. He reminded me of his company's ban on religious programs and pointed out that there were no microwave facilities in Akron to carry such a live television broadcast to the Storer company's transmission tower in Cleveland. It was still the 1950s, when television was live; there was no videotape, and certainly nothing digital. In those days, very few television shows were picked up from locations outside the studio because of the expense and complications of sending a live picture from the camera on the scene to the transmitter on a tower many miles away. The only exceptions were extraordinary news events like a president's inauguration or a World Series. A microwave relay or a high-frequency coaxial cable might be available for picking up a football game in another city, but why go to such expense to get a live feed from a Bible-preaching service in a church?

Naturally, I disagreed. And I had a proposition to make.

I'd pay all the expenses, I finally told the manager, for installing a microwave relay system between Akron and Cleveland, in exchange for the Storer company putting our Sunday church services on the air. And, I added, I would pay for our television time on the Cleveland station.

The manager was astonished. So was I, since I had no idea how I would raise so much money! But he still refused my offer because of his company's policy against religious broadcasts.

I came back to talk with him again the following week, and again on several more occasions, always meeting with firm refusals. Maude Aimee, Wayne, and Leona began keeping a count of my weekly trips to WXEL.

"This is visit number ten to that poor man in Cleveland," Wayne said to me one day as I prepared to set out for the Storer office. "He keeps telling you he can't do it because it's against the company's policy. Don't you believe the man means what he's saying?"

"Sure, I believe him," I replied.

"Then why do you keep bothering him?"

"I'm praying that God will change the policy," I answered, an echo of my father's frequent declaration that "no doesn't mean no when God is saying yes."

After my twelfth visit to the station manager, I asked Maude Aimee, Wayne, and Leona to fast and pray with me for a change in the company's policy. My father had often fasted in prayer for special help from God, and in my own experience I had come to believe strongly in what the Bible says about fasting. In this case, Wayne figured we were talking about missing two or three meals at the most. When the fast went into its third straight day, he grumbled: "Man, even if they change the policy, there won't be any services to send up to Cleveland. We'll all be dead!"

I had fasted for twenty-one straight days before I felt the Spirit of God prompting me to head back up to Cleveland for visit number thirteen. On that day, I gathered Maude Aimee, Wayne, and our little ministry team for prayer. Then I headed out to the parking lot, got into my car, and put the key in the ignition. But before I had started the engine, I sensed a "still, small voice" in my spirit, saying, "Not yet." Romans 8:14 says, "For as many as are led by the Spirit of God, these are the sons of

God," and I have always endeavored to be led by that Spirit. So I sat in my car for a few moments, asking God for more guidance. The guidance I received was quite simple: "Not yet," He said again.

Finally, I retrieved my key, got out of the car, and went back into the office. I called everyone back together and announced, "We're going to pray some more."

"Would to God you'd get on television!" Wayne growled. "You're going to starve us all to death!"

"Wayne, shut up and get down on your knees," I replied cheerfully.

We all knelt and began to pray. We prayed until I felt that strange little burden in my heart lifting. I bid them all good-bye, went out and got in my car, started the engine, and headed north.

I don't know exactly how long it took me to drive from Calvary Temple in Cuyahoga Falls to a certain parking lot in downtown Cleveland, and then to walk from the parking lot to the front door of the building on Euclid Avenue where WXEL had its offices, but my journey was perfectly timed by God. As I reached the door of the building, I almost bumped into a man who was also trying to walk through the door at exactly the same moment. I recognized his face. He was the manager of a radio station in West Virginia whose mother had come to faith in Christ through our meetings in Wheeling years before.

"Mr. Ryan," I said.

"Rex Humbard!" he exclaimed. "What are you doing here in Cleveland?"

"I'm here to tell the manager of this television station that he needs a good religious program."

"I've seen it on that station in Akron," Ryan said, "and you're right: it is a good program. Come on in with me and I'll introduce you to the station manager."

I didn't mention to Ryan that I had already been to see the manager twelve times. The manager didn't mention it either when Ryan introduced us. It turned out that Ryan was now the Storer Broadcasting Company's district supervisor, in charge of several stations in our area, including the one in Cleveland.

In other words, Ryan was the station manager's boss.

We discussed my offer to pay the costs of a microwave relay of our services from Akron to Cleveland in addition to paying for time on the station for Sunday broadcasts.

"I've known Rex and his family for years," Ryan said to the manager. "I think their type of religious program would be good in this area. I want you to clear that time for him and put him on."

Ryan left the room. "How did you meet him?" the manager asked. "Never you mind," I replied. "Just do what he says."

We were on television in Cleveland the following Sunday morning.

God had honored our fasting and prayer, and my obedience to the "still, small voice" of His Spirit. If I had been fifteen seconds earlier or later, I would have failed to connect with Ryan. But God had brought Ryan and me to the same doorstep from miles apart at exactly the same moment. And on top of that, God had changed the policy!

WHATEVER IT TAKES

I drove home elated and announced that a crew of technicians were coming to set up a microwave relay that would carry our Sunday church services to the station in Cleveland.

"Doc, how much is it going to cost us?" Wayne asked, practical as always.

I added up the cost: microwave relay, airtime charges for Cleveland, regular Akron television budget, church operations—and the total was three times more than what we'd been spending.

"We can't afford it," Wayne said. "We can't spend three times more than our present monthly budget just to be on television in Cleveland. We're having a hard enough time making ends meet as it is."

"We've got to do it," I said to him. "This is what we're here to do. The Lord didn't tell us to go forth and preach the Gospel to as many people as we could afford to reach without going into debt. He told us to preach the Gospel to all people."

This became our policy. We would do whatever it took to reach lost souls. We would spend; we would borrow; we would ask for help; we would ask some more. It was not about a spending policy; it was about souls. It was not about a business plan, although a business plan would be fine, but about the far greater priority: reaching lost souls.

We struggled to pay our bill in Cleveland; we struggled every month. It took three years of programs, every Sunday, before we received enough contributions from Cleveland area viewers to cover the cost of our broadcasts there. This, too, would become our pattern. In the next twenty years of working to take the Gospel by television to all of North America, this was our heaviest burden: supporting the program financially in new territories until we attracted enough devoted contributors to cover the costs of broadcasting in those areas. Yet for the sake of souls, we pressed on. We took risks, signed contracts on faith, borrowed—and kept pressing on some more!

Twenty years later, incidentally, I had lunch with the station manager from the Storer station in Cleveland. He informed me that our program by then had been appearing continuously on the station longer than any other, in spite of the fact that the company *still* had a strict policy against religious broadcasts!

I pushed; God pulled. We got our services carried on the Bell system's coaxial cables to stations in Zanesville and Steubenville, Ohio, and then to stations in Parkersburg and Clarksburg, West Virginia. One day I received a phone call from a coal mine operator in Johnstown, Pennsylvania, whom I had never met, a wonderful man named Ben Lingle. He had seen us on television in Cleveland and wanted to know if we could bring our Sunday program into Johnstown. I explained to Ben that our chances of getting an hour of television time on Sunday in Johnstown were doubtful. Even if the local station would sell us the time, paying for the airtime plus the expensive cable charges to bring our program live into Pennsylvania was far beyond our financial reach at the moment.

"Suppose I can get you the time," Ben said, "and supposed I can get my coal company to pay for it, which shouldn't be difficult since I happen to own the company. Then would you bring your program into Johnstown?"

A few days later Ben called me again. "The time is available," he said, "and my company agrees to pay the bills. When can you start feeding that program in here?"

For the next two years, until we began receiving enough donations from our Johnstown audience to cover the costs, Ben's coal company paid the bills from that TV station.

UNDIGNIFIED GOINGS ON

Less than a year after the opening of Calvary Temple, a million people were watching our 11:00 a.m. service each Sunday morning on TV stations in Ohio, Pennsylvania, and West Virginia. We were also doing a local Cleveland station five mornings a week, an evening program in Akron, daily radio programs morning and evening, and my middle-of-the-night program. We had activities and prayer and Bible meetings at our church every night, including an illustrated Bible talk on Saturdays with costumed actors and scenery. We had a dial-a-prayer phone ministry with a new recorded message every day. We had a "spiritual clinic" at our church for two hours every morning, where people with problems came for conversation and prayer with volunteer counselors. We often found as many as three hundred people lined up in the morning waiting for the clinic to open!

Week after week, people found Christ, and their lives began to change through the ministry of our church. One Sunday as I was preaching my sermon before the TV cameras, a man came in through the front door and walked down the middle aisle, followed by a dog. He made his way unsteadily to the platform where I was speaking. It was obvious he had taken a few drinks too many. I paused in my sermon.

> **Week after week, people found Christ, and their lives began to change through the ministry of our church.**

"What can I do for you?" I asked.

"Reverend, I need a little help from God," he replied. "I've been drinking pretty hard, and my wife has been giving me a hard time about it. This morning we started watching you on TV, and my wife started in on me again. So I said to her, 'All right, I'm going over there to talk it over with Rex right now.' I brought my dog with me because he's the only one who can stand me, and here we are."

I looked out at the congregation and said, "All you men who had a drinking problem until you made your peace with God…I want you to stand up and come forward."

More than a hundred men left their seats and moved to the platform. I directed them to gather around the fellow with the alcohol problem and to pray with him. After I led prayer, Wayne guided the man to our counseling room, and I resumed my sermon.

Afterward, a prominent woman in our church announced that she was leaving Calvary Temple; she could not tolerate a pastor who engaged in such undignified goings on during a Sunday service. I didn't try to change her mind. I knew she would never agree that charity, in God's eyes, is much greater than dignity.

Hitting the Road Again

Gradually we extended our live broadcasts on the phone company's cables to more stations in Pennsylvania, then into Indiana and Michigan, giving our Sunday services widespread audiences in the largest heavily populated region of the country. As our unseen television congregation grew in numbers, I felt the urge to travel to the cities and towns where those people watched us and prayed with us on Sundays in their living rooms. I wanted to get together with our viewers in person at a revival meeting on a Tuesday or Thursday evening so they could meet us personally, pray with us, and most importantly, accept Christ as Lord and Savior if they hadn't already!

So we began "television rallies." We climbed into station wagons and buses—Gospel singers and instruments and equipment—and hit the road again, a flashback to the days of my dad's circuit-riding ministry. It was rough going. We would appear at a rally in West Virginia or Indiana, pack up, and drive all night to do our Gospel music program live on the air at the studio in Cleveland at 7:15 the next morning. I kept assuring Maude Aimee and Leona and our weary musicians that someday soon there would be a system of recording TV shows in advance, so we wouldn't have to get out of bed at 4:30 every morning to do that live Cleveland program.

"Oh sure," our musical director Danny Koker joked. "But we'll all be dead from lack of sleep long before those recording things are ever invented!"

Yet God had given me a glimpse of the future. The coming technological revolution, from videotape to satellites, would transform our ability to reach lost souls.

SOMETHING THAT DIDN'T EXIST

Calvary Temple was far too small from the day we opened the doors, and by our first anniversary its inadequacy was painful. We were doing Sunday morning services at 8:30 and 9:30, then a televised service at 11:00, followed by identical services at 3:00 and 7:00 p.m. We considered enlarging the building, but there wasn't enough space to grow into. We considered buying the nearby State Theater, a movie house with 800 more seats than we already had, but 800 seats wouldn't solve our problem. The crowds jamming Calvary Temple every Sunday made it clear that what we really needed was something that didn't exist: a church with at least 5,000 seats. I began to dream of an auditorium that could hold our entire congregation in a single service, designed not just for church but for television, a place from which the Gospel could be broadcast across America and, someday, around the world.

We found the perfect location for a huge church just two miles from Calvary Temple, literally up the street on State Road, near Portage Trail. The owner was eager to sell, but two brothers named Kosar who operated a driving range for golfers on the lot had a lease on the property with eight more years to run. Two previous attempts to buy the lot for a shopping center had been abandoned because the brothers refused to sell their lease.

I visited the owner. The price he quoted me was far too high: $250,000 for sixteen acres. I suspected that he, like a lot of people in Akron, assumed that our church was rolling in money because we were producing TV and radio programs and hiring twenty-two buses to carry people to and from our services every week. So I went to a friend of mine, a real estate broker in Cuyahoga Falls, and asked him to get me an option

117

on the property without revealing to the owner that he was representing our church. I gave the agent enough money to cover the down payment on an option.

"I've got a buyer who wants an option to buy your property," my friend said to the owner, "for $140,000."

The owner grabbed the offer. The real estate broker brought us the option. The owner, when he learned the identity of his buyer, erupted in rage. In spite of the signed document, he refused to release the property to any church. Our friend Clare Conlan was a friend of the owner; he arranged to meet him for lunch at the City Club. In spite of a strict diet for a heart condition, the man decided to indulge himself with a plate of hotcakes. The two men talked about the property deal, but the owner was adamant. "Not for a church," the man insisted. "Not till my dying day."

They parted company. Conlan was miffed but helpless. The man got in his car and headed toward Cleveland, where he planned to attend a Democratic Party event. Across the high-level bridge, in front of St. Joseph Hospital, he suddenly suffered a heart attack. His car plowed into several vehicles on a used-car lot. He was rushed into the hospital, but he was already dead.

Until today, I've never told a soul. But I've often wondered whether people realize the risk they incur when they deliberately stand in God's way.

A Church Made of Cardboard

Now all I had to do was persuade the Kosar brothers to sell their eight-year lease. I spent an evening talking with Mike Kosar in his golf shop on State Road; we got along fine. I asked Mike to figure out how much profit he would clear from operating the driving range over the next eight years—and if it wouldn't be nicer to collect that much money right now, in a payment from our church, than to spend the next eight hot summers

118

cutting all that grass and picking up all those golf balls? The Kosars sold us the lease.

The next few weeks were a whirlwind. We conducted a fund-raising campaign at the church, sold Cathedral of Tomorrow bonds to friends and church members, borrowed here and there, and finally raised enough money to buy the sixteen acres and two adjoining smaller plots that we needed to square off the site for our new church. God even provided the down payment for two houses across the street, which became parsonages: one for Wayne and Leona's family, the other for ours.

With a total of twenty-one acres of land, we were ready to build a church. Ed DeBartolo, a construction man who had just built a shopping center across from our site on State Road, offered to take on the work and obtain the financing for it. But even though he was one of the biggest and most reputable construction contractors in the state, he was dismayed to discover that banks were not willing to lend money for the building of a church—especially a $2 million church! A shopping center or an industrial park? Fine. But a church? No way. "If we had to foreclose," more than one banker asked Ed, "what would we do with a church?"

I hit the road looking for a mortgage. I needed 40 or 50 percent of the construction costs: about $1 million. I went to New York, Los Angeles, Chicago, and Dallas. I talked with banks. I talked with insurance companies. Nobody was interested in helping us.

So I went ahead anyway.

I went to architects to draw up plans according to the building I had visualized: a round church with a huge, round dome, symbolizing the world that our television ministry would reach. Again I met discouraging obstacles. Architects and builders told me that construction of such a large building in a circular shape was impractical, if not impossible. "You can't bend plumbing pipes and air conditioning and heating ducts to fit against a rounded wall," I was told. "You have to have square corners."

So I went to Chicago to visit the outstanding architect A. L. Salzman. He had a reputation as a designer of original and innovative distinction. I explained to Salzman and his three sons, who were associated with him, the concept of the Cathedral of Tomorrow: the domed auditorium with a huge semicircle of five thousand seats, unmarred by supporting pillars. I also told them I had no money; I couldn't find financing from banks or other institutions.

Salzman listened intently. He scribbled notes as I talked. When I was finished, he told me he was interested. He was leaving soon on vacation, and he wanted me to return in two weeks.

When I came back two weeks later, I saw how he had spent part of his vacation. He had taken the cardboard from dress shirts, cut them into small pieces, and used them to build a miniature domed building, the church I had imagined!

Somehow, God had moved in his heart. Salzman turned to his sons. "He's going to build this church," he said, "and we're going to help him."

Salzman couldn't help us with financing, but he had an offer to make: "We will design the building just as you want it designed," he said, "and we'll supervise the construction of it. And we won't ask you for any money until after the building is completely finished and you've been able to secure your mortgage. We'll wait until you have the money to pay us, and we won't expect any payments at all until that time."

All three of his sons began to talk at once.

"But, boss—"

"Boss, do you mean to say that—"

"Boss, we can't do that!"

Salzman looked at his sons and responded in a firm tone. "Don't 'boss' me," he answered. "I've just told him we're going to do it, and we will do it."

The Salzmans kept their promise. They did not ask me for one dollar at any time during the building of the Cathedral of Tomorrow, and they waited patiently for five years afterward without a word of complaint, until I was finally able to secure a mortgage to pay them and our contractors. It was an enormous irony that a Jewish carpenter would build the Cathedral, and I prayed fervently that God would bless them for their unselfishness and willingness to sacrifice on behalf of our ministry.

ONE LITTLE HOLE IN THE GROUND

I finally managed to get from a local bank a verbal promise—nothing in writing—for a one-third turnkey mortgage. This was a loan for one-third of the total cost of the construction, and it would not be given to us until after the building was completed and a key could be turned to open the front door.

Progress! I called together a group of contractors, told them about the promise of the one-third mortgage and about our plans to raise the rest of the construction costs by selling bonds to our church members and friends.

Then I offered them a proposition. "If you'll build the church," I told them, "carry one-third of the costs until after the building is completed. Then I can get that one-third turnkey mortgage from the bank and pay you off. In the meantime, while you're working on the building, I'll be paying you the other two dollars of every three that I owe you. I'll get it as we go along, by selling church bonds...or borrowing wherever I can from time to time."

The contractors agreed. More progress!

Still, however, I lacked the cash to get actual construction under way. I felt sure that our people would start giving generously, and many more bonds could be sold if we could only get the ground broken for the basement and foundation to show folks some real signs of action. By God's grace, a friend lent me $25,000 to get the ball rolling. Inspired, I went to Chicago to see Salzman again.

"Can't we get started with $25,000?" I asked him.

Salzman was sympathetic, but he couldn't conceal his amusement.

"The circumference of the outer wall's foundations is 943 feet," he explained patiently. "For $25,000, the contractors couldn't even dig the holes, let alone pour the concrete and set the steel supports."

I was frantic.

"Couldn't we dig just a few holes," I asked, "and pour a little bit of concrete and set in only a bit of the steel for the time being? When that's done, I'm sure we'll have raised enough new money to do a little more."

Salzman exhibited saintly levels of patience and understanding. Three mornings later, a crane was digging a small hole in the center of the circle staked out for the Cathedral's foundations. It wasn't much of a hole, but it was enough to put pictures of the earth-moving machine in the Akron *Beacon Journal* under a headline that proclaimed "Construction Started on the Cathedral of Tomorrow."

The bonds began to sell, and the little hole grew bigger.

Silent Fireworks

As the walls of the church began to rise, the naysayers gathered.

"You'll never fill a church that big," people said. "There just aren't enough folks who will come here to Akron to support such a huge building."

I decided to show the critics that a big crowd could be attracted to a religious event in our part of the state if it was interesting enough to win widespread attention. A fireworks manufacturer in the city of Hudson was known for staging spectacular pyrotechnic displays at religious festivals in Latin America, with sparkling crosses, Jesus rising in the sky, and flares spelling out messages like "God is the Answer." I wanted an Easter Sunday morning display, going off at 4:00 a.m. from the outdoor drive-in movie theater on State Road near our construction site. But there was a hitch: the township officials would only grant me a permit if the fireworks show was quiet enough for the neighbors to sleep through it.

"Don't worry, Reverend," the fireworks expert told me. "This whole show, including the Resurrection scene, won't make a sound."

Speculation stirred up publicity. Could fireworks be noiseless? We had headlines in Akron, Cleveland, and all over the state.

On the afternoon before the big show, the fireworks man came to me with a suggestion: "A really big number for the grand finale." He wanted to send up "sky searchers."

"They'll make a racket," I replied. "I promised the township officials that we wouldn't make any noise at that hour of the morning, especially on a Sunday morning."

"Oh no," the fireworks man said. "These sky-searcher rockets will light up the whole sky and you'll still be able to hear a pin drop."

Reluctantly, I agreed to his proposal.

Sunday came—and so did the crowds. People from all over the state decided to drive to Cuyahoga Falls to see the spectacle. The Ohio Turnpike and all the roads between Cleveland and Akron were jammed. Our Gospel quartet from Calvary Temple had appeared in Cleveland on Saturday evening and couldn't get to the church in time for our services. At 4:00 a.m. the highway at the drive-in theater was clogged with more than thirty thousand people!

The fireworks show began. It was spectacular—and astonishingly quiet. Burst after burst of light filled the sky. Finally, at the ultimate moment, the sky searchers went up for the grand finale. A deafening explosion shook the whole township.

The fireworks expert was live on the radio with me at the time. "You said they didn't make any racket!" I said. The fireworks man, with no claim to religious faith, replied, "Hell, we've got to get them up there!"

"A man five miles away," the newspaper said, "swore that the Rev. Rex Humbard's 'silent fireworks' made him jump out of his bed."

But that same newspaper story reported that we had caused the biggest traffic tie-up in the history of the county. I had made my point. Several people asked me the following week, "Don't you think you're building that church too *small?*"

No More Bills

For two years we scrimped and saved and begged and borrowed and prayed and wondered where we could get enough money to keep the contractors working. At the same time, we were paying our weekly television bills to keep our Sunday broadcasts on the air. Again and again, we sank into dark discouragement, only to see God come through for us and lift our hearts and spirits.

At one point we got behind by more than $6,000 in our payments to a Pennsylvania station; it was a much higher balance than the station had ever carried on its books. The station owner called his sales manager for an explanation.

"That's Rex Humbard," the sales manager said. "He's having a hard time financially right now."

"Is that the minister who's building that big church near Akron?" the owner asked. "No wonder he's hard-pressed. You tell him that if he'll just scrape up enough money to pay us what he owes us, we won't send him any bills from now on."

When the sales manager relayed the message, I assumed it meant "pay up and get out."

"You don't know the man I work for," the sales manager advised me. "He means that if you pay up now, he'll let you broadcast on his station free of charge from here on in."

It was a fabulous offer, but $6,000 was completely out of reach for me. Where could I find that kind of money *right now?*

Then I thought of Granny Peck. Years before, her poor farmer husband had died and left her penniless. The old man had never belonged to a church, so she could hardly find a denominational minister willing to conduct his funeral. That sad experience led her to join our nondenominational congregation. One day she came to my office and handed me a check for $2,000.

"I sold my farm," she announced. "You folks have been so kind to me. You've been looking after me and picking me up and taking me to church when I had no way of getting there. I've been praying for God to help me financially so I could give you some money for your new church."

The farm, as it turned out, had sold for a quarter-million dollars. Developers would turn the property into an industrial park, and Granny Peck committed to give 10 percent to the church.

"Here's your first tithe," she said to me.

I was amazed. I thanked her, but she wasn't finished with me.

"Now I want to ask you for some advice," she said. She would be receiving regular payments on the farm sale, and she wanted to divide them between her children. But there was a hitch.

"I have one son who lives in Texas," she said. "I never hear from him. I'm not going to give him any of my money. What do you think?"

I reminded her of the biblical story of the prodigal son. "Mrs. Peck, he's still your son," I said. "If you're going to give money to your other children, you should send some to him, too. Look at what we've done to Jesus Christ, and look at the love He still gives us."

Granny Peck nodded. A few months later, when she received the next payment on her farm, she sent $5,000 to her son in Texas. Ten days later he came to Ohio with his wife, and they had a joyous reunion. That son was devoted to his mother for the remaining few years of her life. The kindness and forgiveness that she had shown to him had healed the rift between them.

After that, when I needed $6,000 in a hurry to keep our Sunday services on TV in Pennsylvania, I went to Granny Peck.

She lent me the money without pause, and I wired it to the station immediately.

"Don't thank me," Granny said. "I'll never be able to thank you for the advice you gave me about my son."

The station owner in Pennsylvania kept his promise; he broadcast our services every Sunday free of charge. And for years, his station was the only one in all of North America that never sent us a bill.

* * *

Construction had begun on the Cathedral, we were still holding services in Calvary Temple, and we were in trouble. During a Sunday morning service, I was sitting beside Wayne on the stage as the choir sang, trying to prepare my heart for the sermon I was about to deliver, but I was preoccupied by a different challenge altogether. The contractors required $86,000 by Wednesday; otherwise they would stop work on the new church.

"Where are we going to raise all that money in the next three days?" I asked Wayne.

He cocked his head in that trademark style of his. "Just keep on doing what you've been doing all along," he replied. "Trust in the Lord."

The choir finished. I stood up. "That's just what I'm planning to do," I whispered to Wayne.

I delivered the sermon, then talked from my heart about our hopes and plans for the Cathedral of Tomorrow. I told them I needed their help to pay the bill that was due on Wednesday. At the afternoon service and again in the evening service, I told our people about our need. Our congregation was always comprised mainly of hard-working people of modest means. We had very few major donors. Yet that Sunday night, as we counted the gifts and pledges we had collected in those three services, we found that we had more than the $86,000 we needed! Every single pledge was honored before Wednesday. We paid the contractors, and the work went ahead without pause.

BOTTLES AND BANJOS

I invited Richard Nixon to attend the grand opening of the Cathedral. I had met him years before when our family was holding a month-long revival at the San Pedro Mission Playhouse in California. The facility happened to be in the district where Nixon was running for Congress, and it was the only viable location for a debate. I agreed to give up the Playhouse for that evening if we could open the debate by playing thirty minutes of Gospel music and promoting our revival. Nixon won the debate and the seat in Congress, and I stayed in touch with him over the years. When I next saw him face to face, he was Eisenhower's vice president.

"Do you still have all those whisky bottles and banjos?" he asked.

He remembered our countrified music from the San Pedro Mission, where we used a mallet to hit whisky bottles with various levels of water to get different tones and played sleigh bells and cowbells along with the usual guitar, banjo, mandolin, and bass.

When I invited him to the Cathedral's opening, Nixon agreed. But the *Beacon Journal* got wind of it and rushed to contact the vice president's office. They quizzed his staff about Nixon's knowledge of our financial problems, making it clear that Nixon, if he attended the opening, would get the same kind of bad publicity we were getting. So Nixon reversed his decision, and then the *Beacon Journal* hypocritically claimed that I had invited the vice president but that he declined!

BUILT ON MIRACLES

Preparing the Cathedral for the grand opening was a monumental effort. Maude Aimee worked harder than any of us, selecting the interior decorations and supervising the work of furnishing the auditorium, climbing ladders to check on lighting fixtures, and crawling between rows of seats to correct the fit of floor carpeting. She and I did a daily afternoon radio broadcast for two years while the church was being constructed, interviewing workmen on the site in the winter cold and the summer heat, describing to our listeners the progress of the work. Our afternoon broadcast became such a popular daytime feature in Ohio that our station in Cleveland kept it on the air for nine years after the Cathedral was completed!

Wayne often said that the Cathedral of Tomorrow was not built on money; it was built on miracles. Without furnishings, the building cost $2.5 million—in 1958 dollars. It was the largest dome-roof house of worship in the world, with a semicircle of 5,400 seats facing a 168-foot-wide stage. We could never have built such a church on our own. God had to build it for us.

More than 60,000 visited the Cathedral of Tomorrow on the day of our grand opening on May 24, 1958. That morning, we staged a parade of our youth groups along State Road from Calvary Temple to the Cathedral. That afternoon I served as guide for a tour of the facilities before a live television audience. It wasn't evident, but we had actually created an enormous television studio. The cameras showed the huge, 100-foot-tall lighted cross under the largest domed roof of any church in the world. The vaulting span of the dome was 220 feet, with no interior supports marring the expanse of its 38,000 square feet of rounded ceiling—82 feet wider than the famous dome of the Cathedral of Florence in Italy. The dome of the Cathedral of Tomorrow, made of wood four inches thick, was called "the wood-engineering marvel of the century" by the art editor of the Cleveland *Plain Dealer*. We had designed the floor to hold miles of cable out of view. Decades later, Radio City Music Hall would have to be remodeled to achieve the same effect. We were half a century ahead of our time!

We had nurseries for babies and toddlers, 154 Sunday school rooms, a library, and a prayer room for counseling new converts. The first speaker at our afternoon program was the architect A. L. Salzman, who attended opening day ceremonies with his sons and their families. As Salzman concluded his talk, one of his young grandsons called out to him loudly: "Grandpa, who's the rabbi here?"

That night at our Bible service, more than 7,500 people filled the Cathedral, and thousands more had to be turned away. Families came in cars, buses, and trucks from all over the Midwest, from West Virginia and Kentucky, from Pennsylvania and New York.

It had been just five years since my decision to stay behind in Akron and start a church with sixty-five dollars in my pocket.

* * *

My father was delighted. He lived to see the Cathedral of Tomorrow dedicated and our nationwide television ministry launched. Shortly before his death, I described to him the areas of the Midwest and the border states that we were then reaching on Sundays. His eyes sparkled.

"Rex, do you realize," he said, "you are reaching in one hour more people than I preached to in all my fifty-three years as a minister?"

He died four days before Christmas in 1959, passing the evangelistic torch to me.

My mother continued standing with us. She sat next to me on the stage at the Cathedral of Tomorrow every Sunday morning until she died in 1983. My parents' bodies finally failed, but their fervor for souls never waned.

SEVEN

A Dome for a Home

The grand opening of the Cathedral of Tomorrow might have made a triumphant ending for our story, but as it turned out, it only set the stage for a massive crisis. As Maude Aimee often said, when your work for God is going well, watch out for the devil! That's when he gets jealous and starts to work his hardest against you.

The opening of our magnificent new church apparently stirred up resentment among some of Akron's influential businessmen and bankers. So while we had built the Cathedral counting on the mortgage loan for one-third of the construction costs, it had wound up at around $800,000, to be paid to the architect and the contractors, who had so generously agreed to wait till I received the promised loan before collecting the balance owed to them.

With the Cathedral open, I called our bank to ask about arrangements for payment of our mortgage loan. Sorry, they said; they had decided to break the promise. The loan I had been planning and depending on would not be forthcoming. There was no explanation. Even though our architects and contractors had accepted the promise as security when they set out to build the Cathedral of Tomorrow, there would be no mortgage loan. And that was that.

Suddenly we had nearly $1 million in debt for unpaid construction bills.

When the news broke across the local business community, the contractors were strongly advised to sue. Only two of the smallest subcontractors, people I had never dealt with personally, filed suit. Their claims amounted to $67,000, just a small fraction of our total debt. Still, the mechanics' liens they filed against the church damaged our credit rating and stirred up a storm of newspaper headlines: "Rex Can't Pay for His Cathedral" and "New Church in Financial Troubles." The bad publicity frightened many of the good bond investors. In a single week we received requests for repayment of nearly a quarter-million dollars' worth—bonds which weren't due to be paid until nine or, in some cases, fifteen years later. I had no choice; I went to our congregation and asked them to buy additional bonds in order to pay the worried investors.

Then I called a meeting of all the contractors who had worked on the building. There were thirty-two of them; they came with their lawyers. My office at the Cathedral was so crowded for that meeting that there was hardly any standing room.

"You fellows want your money," I began, "and I want to give it to you. But the bank isn't coming through on its commitment to me. I know you must have gone to that bank and gotten verification of their commitment two years ago before you went ahead on this job. So you know I'm telling you the truth. You've been good enough to wait until I can work this thing out. But there are two men here who didn't wait. They filed liens against me, and that's why I'm in trouble now, on account of the publicity caused by those liens. I suggest that the first thing we should do today is get rid of those two men. Then we'll talk."

The leading contractor, a builder who had more money at stake than any of the others, stood up and said to the two subcontractors, "How much do you two have coming to you? Sixty-seven thousand dollars? I'll buy your notes at a 15 percent discount."

The two men, embarrassed and uncomfortable, accepted his offer and hurried out of the room.

Then, before I could speak, the leading contractor addressed the group.

"Gentlemen, we told the reverend that we'd wait for our money until he gets a mortgage," he began. "I intend to keep my word, and I think all of you ought to keep yours. I'm suggesting that we take one mortgage for the entire amount owed to us. Whenever Rex is able to pay us any money at all, we'll take it, and we'll carry the rest of the debt until he can pay it off, no matter how long that may be."

Another contractor stood to speak, "That's all right with the rest of us, isn't it, boys?"

There were nods all over the room.

I looked around, somewhat stunned. I saw Catholics and Protestants and Jews. This was clearly not about sectarianism. God was doing something. These men knew, as I did, that standing beside me in this time of crisis might antagonize some of the local bankers and financiers whom they depended on for support in their business dealings. But they still refused to turn their backs on me. As I shook hands with each of them, listening to their warm words of encouragement, I was thinking how blessed we were by God when He selected such good men to build our church.

And their word was indeed their bond. These loyal contractors waited patiently and uncomplainingly for the next five years while I tried everywhere, without success, to raise a mortgage.

Those were five long and dreary years of discouraging days and sleepless nights. We prayed for strength and faced one trial after another. Banks complained to state securities authorities in Columbus because members of our congregation and our TV audience were withdrawing money from their savings accounts to invest in our church's bonds. We finally had to stop selling bonds until our debts were cleared up, which left us no source of revenue except Sunday offerings from our congregation and donations from our TV audience. Gifts to our TV ministry had to go toward payment of our TV stations. So I had to give up any hope of extending our television network during those grim years.

This crisis came so early that we had not yet installed air conditioning in the Cathedral of Tomorrow; and with funding severely diminished, there was no way to install such a system. So for nearly five years, we soldiered on through the hot-weather months. The heat was often unbearable in our Sunday school classrooms. Teachers often led children outdoors to shady places on the lawn, or downstairs to a cool corner of the basement…and smiled through it all.

It seemed that help would never come, until one day when help came from a most unexpected source: Jimmy Hoffa.

THE HOFFA CONNECTION

Our congressman at that time representing Ohio's 14th District, was William H. Ayres, a Methodist Republican who often attended services at the Cathedral. The congressman, a close personal friend of my lawyer, was familiar with our troubles, which he frequently discussed with me.

When Bill Ayres ran for reelection in 1962, he was strongly opposed in Akron by the local leaders of Jimmy Hoffa's Teamsters Union, on orders from Hoffa himself, who regarded Ayres as too conservative. The Teamsters were a strong force in Ohio politics, but Bill managed to regain his seat in the House of Representatives despite Hoffa's opposition.

A few months later, Attorney General Robert F. Kennedy—still carrying on his longtime feud with Hoffa—managed to push through Congress a federal law requiring all union leaders to be bonded by insurance companies, supposedly for the protection of union members against the misuse or theft of union funds. Hoffa found himself unable to obtain such a bond, apparently thanks to Kennedy's influence, so he faced the threat of being removed from the presidency of his union.

Bill Ayres, in spite of the opposition he had faced at Hoffa's hands, was outraged by Kennedy's scheme; he saw it as a bald-faced violation of Hoffa's constitutional rights. Ayres demanded an investigation into the question of why Hoffa had been denied a bond. Ayres's colleagues in Congress were impressed, particularly because he was advocating for his old adversary. So Ayres's resolution received strong support in the House, and suddenly, mysteriously, Jimmy Hoffa found that he could obtain a bond with no trouble at all. The Ayres resolution, and the uproar that came with it, had had the desired effect.

Soon Hoffa was sitting in Ayres's office, thanking him for his help.

"Don't thank me," the congressman replied. "I wasn't trying to do you any favors. Your people tried to defeat me last November. I just got mad because anybody should have the right to obtain a bond if he hasn't been found guilty on criminal charges. The members of the House agreed with me, so if you want to thank anybody, thank the members of the House of Representatives."

"I'll do that," Hoffa replied. "I'm going to write a letter to each one of them. But isn't there something I can do to express my gratitude to you?"

"There's nothing you can do for me," Bill Ayres answered. But then in a God-ordained moment that would shape our television ministry for decades to come, the congressman had an idea. He offered Hoffa an alternative.

"There's a young preacher in Akron who built a big church there,"

Ayres told Hoffa, "and he can't raise a mortgage to pay off his contractors. He's been doing a lot of good things for a lot of people. Do you think your union's pension fund might give him a mortgage?"

"Why not?" Hoffa replied. "If it looks all right, we'll give him a mortgage."

Ayres passed the news on to his friend, my lawyer Charlie Iden, who promptly talked it over with me.

"Would you take a mortgage loan from Jimmy Hoffa?"

He didn't need to tell me that a lot of people strongly disapproved of Hoffa. It would get me a lot of publicity I didn't want.

"I'll take a mortgage from anybody," I said without hesitating. "As for the publicity, it couldn't be any worse than the publicity I've already gotten."

A few days later I walked into the Edgewater Beach hotel in Chicago to meet with Jimmy Hoffa.

Of all the celebrities I've met in my lifetime, I have never talked with anybody who had a quicker and more penetrating intelligence or more easy poise and assurance than this two-fisted truck driver turned union boss. He was kind and polite, but he wasted no time getting to the point of our discussion.

Our lawyer had already delivered our financial statement, but he asked for another look. Now, watching him glance at the figures, I had the feeling that neither the chairman of the board at General Motors nor the president of the Chase Manhattan Bank could read a balance sheet faster than this unassuming man sitting before me. He wrote a few notes on a pad of paper, called in an auditor, showed him the notes, and said to him, "Check these assumptions I've made and see if they're correct."

I have no idea what those assumptions were.

Somewhere a phone rang and an assistant approached. Someone was calling from Puerto Rico and needed to talk with Hoffa.

"Excuse me, Reverend," Hoffa said. "These guys have been indicted, and I've told them not to call me anymore."

He picked up the phone and unleashed an astonishing storm—yelling, cursing, raving. When I thought he couldn't possibly holler anymore, he hollered some more. He called the man names. He kept yelling. Finally he shouted, "Don't you call me one more time. If you do, I'm going to push every last one of you out of the union and put new men in. You've called me three times; now don't call me again."

He hung up the phone.

"Excuse me, Reverend," Hoffa said quietly. "I'm sorry. That's the only thing they understand."

Then the auditor returned and affirmed the boss's "assumptions."

"Reverend," Hoffa announced, "you've got your mortgage."

But I would need to come back the next morning, he explained, to present my case at a meeting of the pension fund's board members.

"They're a good group of men," he assured me, "and you'll enjoy meeting them."

He followed me out into the hallway.

"I've watched your programs on television," he said. "I want you to know that I feel this is the finest investment we've ever made. This isn't just a mortgage, as far as I'm concerned. It's an investment in a great cause."

And so it was that Jimmy Hoffa's Teamsters Union pension fund gave the Cathedral of Tomorrow a mortgage loan of $1.2 million, after we had spent five solid years trying to raise money from most of the leading banks and lending institutions in the country.

In later years, we would actually go back to the Teamsters when we needed more financial help. They helped us buy color video equipment, for example. We had to switch to color or a number of stations would refuse to carry our programs. (We donated our old black-and-white cameras to Kent State University.) Even though the cameras had a life expectancy of five years, they gave us a twenty-five-year loan on them. The Teamsters never once refused a request to increase our mortgage. At one point it was $5.5 million, yet we never missed a single payment. Our relationship with union officials was always warm and friendly. Nobody could criticize Jimmy Hoffa in my presence. I was proud of his friendship with me.

Giving Something Back

Years later, after Hoffa had been released from jail, I visited him. Security was tight; I had to pass a number of checkpoints. Finally I was with him.

We talked about prison; he opened a closet and told me his jail cell had been hardly any larger than that, but he had exercised diligently.

"I wasn't going to let them get me down," he said.

Then he asked me the inevitable question, "Reverend, how can I help you?"

"Mr. Hoffa, I don't want anything," I replied, the first time I had ever been able to say that to him. "I just came here to pray for the man who did something for me."

I laid my hands on him and prayed for him; then we shook hands and I left.

It was the last time I ever saw him. He disappeared in 1975. His successor, Jackie Presser, told me that Hoffa had been murdered, his body placed in a car and crushed in a Detroit junkyard.

Presser had been involved in all of our mortgage arrangements, and we became friendly over the years. When Presser was diagnosed with cancer, I went to see him in a Cleveland hospital. His son was standing in the hallway, keeping people out of the room because his father was so ill.

The son and I talked for a few moments, then I heard Presser calling from his bed.

"Is that Rex Humbard? It sounds like Rex Humbard!"

He invited me in. "What can I do for you?" he asked.

"I don't want anything," I replied. "I came here to pray for you."

I prayed, he thanked me, and I left, grateful that I could give something back after all those years.

A MULE IN THE WELL

With that first loan from the Teamsters in 1963, we paid our contractors and the Salzmans every dollar that we had owed them—and for which they had waited so patiently—for so many years. Then came the headlines: "Jimmy Loves Rex" and "Teamsters Give Loan to Humbard After Banks Reject Him." I looked at the publicity and decided to think of it as a small price to pay for the help I so desperately needed. At times like that I reminded myself that Jesus Christ was the most criticized man who ever walked the earth.

It had been a long, hard five years. But like the mule who fell into a well in that old Arkansas joke—when the farmer decided to give up on him and simply fill in the well with dirt—we just kept shaking off the dirt, tromping it down under our feet, and rising a little higher. When the farmer had finally filled the well with dirt, when we had finally shaken off five years of disappointment and disapproval, the mule and Rex Humbard both stepped out of the hole and walked away from it!

Nobody can cover up God's work, I've often said.

Nobody can cover up God's work, I've often said. Finally, with our old debts paid off and consolidated by the new loan from this kind man whom many people frowned upon, we began working to build up a bigger and wider-reaching television ministry. Soon we covered all of the United States and Canada.

To meet people who were watching us every Sunday on TV and to reap the harvest of conversions from the seed of faith we had sown through our broadcasts, we began to travel widely by air to monthly rallies of our television followers in distant cities—a jet-age version of the earliest rallies we had produced in the bus-and-truck era.

It was a new way of pioneering, and the new stagecoach of choice was a twenty-one-passenger Vickers Viscount turbojet that we purchased from United Airlines in 1968. It was a step up from our original aged Cessna, which we called *Hezekiah* after the Old Testament king who faced death but got a fifteen-year extension by pleading with God. We crisscrossed the continent.

Our rallies around the country were enormously effective in solidifying viewers' decisions for Christ. In the four years beginning in January 1970 (until the 1974 national fuel shortage curtailed our travels), we ministered in person to more than 646,000 people. More than 80,000 professed their commitment to Christ as Lord and Savior.

I took a call from a man in a hospital in Charlevoix, on the upper peninsula of Michigan. He had suffered a heart attack, he had a life-threatening blood clot, and he wanted me to pray for him.

"How about the inner man?" I asked him. "How is your soul?"

"Oh, it's only my body that needs help from God," he replied. "My soul is all right. I came forward and saved my soul five years ago, at your rally in Traverse City!"

We prayed together on the phone. When I wished him well and hung up, I remembered that night when we landed our plane at Traverse City. The weather was terrible, rainy and foggy. When we made our descent, the visibility was so poor that we were still undecided about trying to make a landing. At the last moment of choice, we agreed to take the gamble and managed to put the plane down on the runway safely. That decision led to the salvation of at least one soul!

* * *

Our ministry kept growing. At the Cathedral of Tomorrow, we developed a Sunday school with forty-four departments and 156 teachers and directors, with classes for every age group. We developed an extensive youth ministry and a visitation program for reaching out to the community's shut-ins in institutions, hospitals, rest homes, and prisons. I began thinking about establishing our own pleasant, friendly living quarters for elderly people who loved our ministry. And finally, after a decade of thinking, dreaming, praying, and planning, we opened the Cathedral Apartments with the help of federal government financing. There were few decent housing projects for senior citizens at that time. The Cathedral Apartments were right on our church property—a cylindrical twelve-story brick building offering the elderly dignity and privacy as well as proximity to our ministry services.

We also set up a covered walkway to connect the Cathedral to a large building across the parking lot. This facility housed our ministry offices, the twenty-four-hour prayer room, our video production area, and the Cathedral Buffet restaurant. The Buffet was crucial to meeting the needs of our staff and various groups in our church. And rather than let the restaurant sit idle when staff or church groups weren't using it, we opened it to the public. It was our first commercial venture designed to bring money into the television ministry, but it would not be our last.

LIFE BEFORE TECHNOLOGY

We were ready before the technology was ready. Television had a limited range in the early days, but when videotape was finally developed, we were already prepared with a program to record! It's difficult to imagine today, in the Internet age, the breathtaking miracle that videotape was. You could record the images and sounds of a Sunday morning church service in the Cathedral of Tomorrow and actually play it back for broadcast at a later date, with perfect reproduction. The potential was mind-boggling. We could tape each service, make hundreds of duplicates of the recording, and send them to TV stations anywhere. Amazing!

We had already established a cyclical "bicycling" system. We shipped a kinescope of our program each week to a station in another city, they aired it, then shipped it on to the next city in the chain. When videotape made recording, editing, and duplication more efficient, we were able to begin with the taping of the service on a Sunday morning and end with the broadcast of the same service on TV stations across the continent exactly three weeks later. We found that God could work just as powerfully through a recorded service after three weeks as He could through the printed pages of the Bible after thousands of years. God's power to heal was the same; God's power to save was the same. And the distribution of videotaped services dramatically multiplied the number of lost souls we could reach in any week.

Of course, even with technology catching up to us, finances typically lagged behind. In each new city, we had to go into the red, losing money every week for the first two or three years. I looked at a map of North America, and my heart ached for the millions of lost people in some three hundred television markets we hadn't yet reached, but my heart also dreaded the cost of airtime in those areas. The debt, even if we could find a lender, would be staggering.

Of course there was another, much easier way to plan a television ministry. We could stop at fifty self-supporting stations, sit back, relax, preach the Gospel on TV every Sunday, enjoying a large widespread audience with no financial problems. That, however, was never on our radar. Every day of my life I thought about lost souls: where they were, how to reach them, what to do to bring the Gospel before them, how to win them to Christ. The vision to bring the message of Jesus Christ via television to all people everywhere burned in my soul.

God, even more passionate about reaching the lost than I was, helped us, often in strange ways. In 1968 we were on sixty-eight stations, mostly in the Midwest. We had never been seen in many of the states of the East, the South, and the Pacific Coast. We were already deep in debt; audiences in most of our existing stations weren't covering costs yet.

One Sunday I asked our television audience to pray with me that someday soon we might be able to be seen in all of the fifty states. It was an audacious dream, but I was determined to head in that direction.

A few days later, a wealthy businessman from Minnesota came to the Cathedral of Tomorrow to talk with me. He had been watching our programs, he was impressed, and he wanted to know how much money it would take to fulfill the dream of going on at least one station in each of the states where we were not yet seen. It didn't take long to come up with an answer: we would need thirty-three additional stations. The cost was astronomical.

But my visitor from Minnesota was undaunted. He would underwrite all thirty-three stations until they became self-supporting, he said, putting up a sum of money I could never have raised by myself in those days. I was stunned, and grateful, and I accepted the offer quickly.

We immediately began arranging to buy time on those thirty-three stations, bringing our network to a grand total of 101. For the first time, we were truly nationwide!

A few weeks later, we staged a rally in Minnesota. Our new sponsor visited with us afterward. He had a few agenda items he wanted to go over, a few changes he wanted us to make in our programs. Altar calls, for example, were too "old-fashioned." Our interdenominationalism concerned him too; he wanted us to align with his denomination and point our television audience to the churches of that group.

I listened politely, thanked him for the help he had been giving, and explained that I couldn't preach the Gospel according to any one particular sectarian interpretation. I simply wanted everybody to believe in Jesus Christ. It made no difference if people in our TV audience joined the Lutherans or the Baptists, the Catholics or the Methodists, the Presbyterians or the Pentecostals, as long as they accepted Christ and lived according to His teachings.

Our benefactor quickly departed, taking his money with him. I never heard from him again.

Now, however, I had thirty-three new television stations that I couldn't pay for. I would never have signed contracts for all that airtime—adding more than $15,000 *per week* to our already heavy budget—if the gentleman from Minnesota hadn't pledged his support. But he was gone, and I was stuck with the bill. We had asked the Lord to put the Cathedral of Tomorrow on television in every state in America, and our prayers had been answered. But we certainly hadn't expected God to spread our evangelistic coverage from coast to coast until we were able to pay for it!

Still, I didn't think in terms of backing away. I could only think in terms of thirty-three cities' worth of lost souls. I made up my mind to find some way of sustaining our Sunday program in those thirty-three new states—raising more money, in fact, to reach even more areas of North America. We were already too deep in debt to borrow large additional sums from banks or other lending companies. Finally, we decided

144

to do what other churches, Christian organizations, and educational institutions were doing on a large scale to support their work: we made plans to establish a fund-raising department at the Cathedral of Tomorrow. This team would solicit private loans, bequests, and other kinds of financial aid from friends in our church membership and in our widespread television congregation who wanted to help us advance our mission.

Early in 1969 we organized the Cathedral of Tomorrow's Stewardship Division, with a staff of traveling solicitors who visited our followers all over the country, offering contribution opportunities and investment plans that would support our work. Investments included interest-paying bonds and notes, annuity trust plans, life estate plans which guaranteed a lifetime income in return for bequests in wills, and various other attractive offers. We found devout Christians everywhere who were happy to have the opportunity to invest in God's work.

The system was carefully crafted on a seven-year repayment plan, following a long-term program that would enable us to meet future payments on bonds and notes through income from bequests and endowments. Meanwhile, over the same seven-year period, as our expanding television network became self-supporting, we would reduce our debts and eliminate our deficit spending. Finally, with God's help and the continued support of our widespread television congregation, we would be able to carry out the dream of taking the Gospel into all the world.

Our launch of a formal fund-raising effort couldn't have come at a more opportune time. Over the past twelve years we had met with stiff resistance everywhere in the television industry when we tried to expand our TV network. I had to beg station managers for the privilege of buying an hour of their time on Sunday mornings. But in 1969, everything suddenly changed. The broadcasting industry finally acknowledged the warm reception we were getting from our growing audiences and began welcoming us into their programming lineups. We were suddenly flooded with offers of choice Sunday morning hours on desirable channels in new locations.

During the next year, with funds raised by our Stewardship Division, we added more than a hundred new stations to our network. *Parade* magazine ran a story about us in Sunday newspapers across the country. It began: "What American TV program appears on the most stations? You might guess *Bonanza*. Or, perhaps, Johnny Carson's *Tonight Show*. Wrong, both times. The program on the most stations, 242 of them in the U.S. and Canada, is Rex Humbard's show—an hour-long Sunday religious service that's known formally as 'The Cathedral of Tomorrow.'" By the end of 1971, our program—God's show, not mine—was being seen on more than 350 television stations all over North America, a network covering virtually all the English-speaking areas of the continent.

And God had accomplished this incredible expansion—nearly a hundred new stations a year for three consecutive years—through the investments of faithful friends who lent us money because they believed in our mission and wanted to help us fulfill it as quickly as possible. If we had waited until our accumulated weekly donations could finance our program on new stations a few slow steps forward at a time, it might have taken us more than fifteen years to do what we did in three. Thanks to loyal church members and television followers pitching in and letting us use their investments, we gained a weekly Sunday audience estimated at more than 20 million—and far sooner than we had ever hoped or even dared to pray for.

We had loads of short-term debt, but we never missed a payment on the Cathedral of Tomorrow mortgage. We never missed an interest payment on our bonds and notes. We paid our television bills faithfully, even when they crested at $6 million a year. By 1976 we would begin to receive an income from the bequests and annuities, which would repay the loans from our loyal supporters, and our widespread television ministry would be self-supporting.

The future looked bright.

But there were grim times ahead.

Girdles for God

As our television costs rose, I was eager to try new ways to raise money. In addition to operating the financially successful Cathedral Buffet, we took on a few other commercial business sidelines, which earned us some criticism in the Akron *Beacon Journal*, but I didn't mind. The Baptist Church owned Burlington Mills. The Mormon Church owned office buildings and businesses all over the world. The Catholic Knights of Columbus owned the land under Yankee Stadium. Paul the apostle made and sold tents to help support his ministry.

We decided to make and sell girdles.

In the '60s, when girdles were still in fashion, we bought the Real Form Girdle Company in Brooklyn. "Rock of Ages Rests on Firm Foundation," one newspaper headline read. We bought the company on a bank loan without a penny of our church's money; the company repaid the loan and brought our television ministry more than a quarter-million dollars in the first year. I had made a solemn promise to God that I would never use one nickel of the money donated to our church in a commercial investment. It was a promise I never broke. When pantyhose began to replace girdles in the clothing market, we sold the company.

We also got into the video production business, something a lot "closer to home." To produce videotaped recordings of our Gospel services for rebroadcast all over North America, we built the best-equipped TV recording studios between New York and Hollywood. With state-of-the-art technology and highly skilled workers, we were able to organize

Cathedral Tele-Productions and make TV commercials for Firestone, Eastman Kodak, Cadillac, Buick, and other customers whose payments subsidized our ministry. The clients loved us because we didn't rush them in and out of the studios like the studios did in New York and L.A. We gave them time. Harvey Firestone liked to come watch the crew make a commercial and preview the finished product without a delay. He and I developed a wonderful fellowship that way.

Then we were given the opportunity to buy, at a small fraction of its appraised value, the vacant, almost brand-new, fully equipped buildings and thirty-two-acre campus of Mackinac College on beautiful Mackinac Island. The island is a beautiful vacation resort on Lake Huron in upper Michigan; the college had been built and briefly operated by the Moral Re-Armament movement. As I prayed about the offer, I felt led to make the purchase and reestablish Mackinac as a four-year Christian college for young men and women, and to use the handsome facilities in the summer months as a family vacation center devoted to Christian spiritual development. The purchase made financial sense. Immediately after we bought the campus, we were offered a million-dollar profit to sell it to another buyer who wanted to develop it as a vacation resort. It would have been a quick, easy million dollars, but God had told me to buy the college, not to sell it.

A few months later, John W. Galbreath, the contractor and real estate developer from Columbus, Ohio, turned over to us the twenty-three-story downtown office building in Akron's Cascade Plaza. We paid the bargain price of $10 million, with no down payment. The income from this building would help support our college, where we hoped someday to train missionaries and television evangelists.

The great day of worldwide spiritual and moral reawakening was coming closer!

FAMILY PICTURE

Meanwhile, the Humbard family was growing. Shortly after the opening of the Cathedral of Tomorrow, Maude Aimee and I celebrated another blessed event: the birth of our daughter Elizabeth on October 1, 1959. Three years to the day later, God gave us our third son, Charley. By the time Liz was eighteen months old, she was singing on one of our radio programs. In her teens she became a featured soloist in our services. Charley followed in my footsteps and began playing the guitar.

Our eldest sons made us grateful and proud when they decided to join us in our work at the Cathedral of Tomorrow. As a teen, Rex Jr. had worked with the church maintenance crew; he became interested in the technical work of our video operations and eventually came to direct our TV camera operators and the entire production effort, with his brother Don serving beside him in the control booth. Eventually, both young men moved into management positions in the ministry's business offices. They also managed and staged our rallies in various cities across North America, besides appearing in our Sunday programs as members of the Humbard Family Singers!

Rex Jr. married Suzy and gave us three grandchildren: Rex Humbard III ("Rexie"), Michael Richard, and Suzanna. Don married Sue and gave us three granddaughters: Donna Sue, Aimie Melissa, and Susan Rae.

One of the big attractions at each of our television rallies and in each week's television broadcast was our musical group, the Humbard Family Singers. I had seen the power of a family singing Gospel music while I was growing up on the road with my father's ministry; we continued that tradition with my own children (and eventually grandchildren) as well as with various close friends who added talented vocals and instrumentation. Countless people were initially drawn to our ministry because of the music. Many longtime members of the Cathedral and lifetime viewers of our program were first attracted not by my preaching but by our unique "family ministry" of music. As each new child and grandchild came along, we added to our group, receiving greater and greater enthusiasm from our viewers!

Ministering as a family became our response to the growing tragedy of the fractured family in modern society. Sometimes we had as many as fifteen of us onstage together—even the very small children sang—and it was this "family picture" that was beloved not only in North America but in other nations when we eventually began broadcasting overseas. Years later, as our ministry expanded across South America, Catholic priests thanked me for our family approach to ministry. Young people in their countries were beginning to return to the church because of the example of the Humbard family.

Prayer Is the Key

At the heart of our ministry for years was the Prayer Key Family. It was birthed by the Spirit of God on our way to a rally in Chattanooga. Several of us—family and staff—were traveling together, and in the course of our conversation, someone mentioned that prayer is the key to membership in God's family. Maude Aimee began spontaneously singing the old Gospel song "Prayer Is the Key, and Faith Unlocks the Door." That did it. The idea for the Prayer Key Family exploded on us. We would send each new member a small key as a reminder to pray whenever he reached for his key ring. We would also send each member a sticker bearing the phone number of our twenty-four-hour Cathedral Prayer Group. A member of the Prayer Key Family pledges to pray daily for the salvation of lost souls, to fast one meal hour each week (lunch on Wednesday was what I suggested), and to give a monthly gift in support of our evangelistic work around the world. We would gather each week during our television program and would pray together over all the needs that had been sent or called in to our ministry during the week. We put a Prayer Key table on the stage of the Cathedral, and each Sunday it was piled high with requests for prayer from every corner of the globe. My family and I would gather around the table every week during the service to pray together—a worldwide prayer meeting!

From the day I first invited our viewers to join the Prayer Key Family, the response was overwhelming. Thousands committed to stand with us, and thousands more joined us each month. The Prayer Key Family became a strong and deep spiritual force, uniting people everywhere in Christ and in partnership with our ministry. A woman in Toronto wrote to say that she, her husband, her daughter in Florida, and her son in California were all members, all joining together on Sunday mornings for prayer with the Prayer Key Family. Such transcontinental stories became commonplace over the years.

To this day, I receive a big bundle of mail from Tokyo every two weeks. It comes from John Sakurai, our Tokyo ministry director, who gathers all the prayer requests from our Prayer Key Family members across Japan. He and the ministry staff there answer the mail, send Christian literature, visit people in hospitals, then forward me the letters. I faithfully lay my hands on the letters and pray for the people who wrote them, even though I can't read a word of Japanese. I trust God to know what those people need. In our ministry offices here in the U.S., I observe exactly the same practice. I pray over every letter we've received from people in need. We're all family. I don't care about a person's denomination or doctrine; I care about their trust in Jesus Christ, and their dependence on God to meet their needs. That's all! That has always been the essence of the Prayer Key Family.

There is spiritual power in the kind of commitment that Prayer Key

Family membership represented. One morning I walked into our church offices and our receptionist advised me that a woman from West Virginia had called three times already that day, asking to talk to Rex Humbard. When I returned the call, the woman told me that she had been a member of our Prayer Key Family for twenty-six years.

"I have prayed every day of my life for our ministry," she said—and I noted that she said "our" ministry, not "your" ministry—"and every month I've sent a gift. It wasn't much some months, but I've sent a gift every month all of these years, because I want God's message to go out, and I want to be a part of it. One time, I didn't have anything but a quarter, and I got a piece of cardboard—"

I interrupted her. "Let me tell you the rest of that story," I said. "You took that piece of cardboard, you got a needle and thread, and you sewed it onto that cardboard. Then you added some paste to keep it from getting loose. You wrote a note that said, 'I'm a member of the Prayer Key Family, and this is all I can do this month.' Then you put it in an envelope and mailed it."

The woman was astonished. "How in the world can you know that?"

"Ma'am," I replied, "that's the only money I ever received for God's work sewed onto cardboard and stuck with paste!"

But the woman was calling with a different agenda.

"I'm going home to be with the Lord," she told me. "I'm in the bed now, and I can't even get up."

"I'm so sorry," I said. "But you never know, I might beat you there."

"No," she insisted, "the Lord told me I was coming home."

"Well, I want to pray for you," I said.

"You can pray for me," she replied, "but don't pray that I'll stay, because the Lord told me it's time to come home!"

She was ready to go!

So why was she calling? Finally, she gave me the surprising answer:

"I've been a member of the Prayer Key Family for twenty-six years, but now I'm not going to be there. I reckon you'll have to get somebody to take my place."

Her role in God's work had assumed such a place of importance in her heart and life that she wanted someone to stand in her position when she was gone!

This has been typical of people involved with our Prayer Key Family down through the years. I couldn't help but think of this phenomenon when I visited a Catholic church in Jerusalem years ago and saw an enormous painting of a person holding a big cross in his hand. Right behind him was another person holding another cross, and right behind that individual was another one, and so on. The line of people curved into the distance. Under the painting was an inscription of Christ's words: "Take up your cross and follow me." I wanted our ministry to faithfully carry that cross, and generations of Prayer Key Family members did exactly that.

Over the years I've met Prayer Key Family members from Harrisburg to Hollywood, from Alaska to the Amazon. In the Tala leper colony in the Philippines, our TV crew was greeted by a woman who emerged beaming from a wretched hut holding our *Prayer Key Family New Testament*, the only Bible in the colony. We saw Indians in Paraguay living as they have for thousands of years along a river bank, without any modern conveniences, but watching a small battery-operated television set and joining with our global family at prayertime during our program every week! Prayer Key Family members all over the world knew what prayer was; we had prayed for each other. We were family. Shaking hands with the Guirnee Indians of Paraguay was virtually the same as shaking hands with people at the back of Cadle Tabernacle in Indianapolis.

153

Worthwhile but Wrong?

We had enjoyed our greatest-ever year of ministry in 1972. We had burst the borders of the North American continent that fall, beginning weekly broadcasts in Australia, the Philippines, and—with voiceover dubbing—Japan. Our worldwide television network stood at nearly four hundred stations. We had just begun our first semester of classes at Mackinac Christian College. We had built, just adjacent to our church facility, the 750-foot Cathedral Tower, destined to be the tallest building in Ohio. When completed, it would be crowned by the transmitter for our own ultrahigh-frequency TV station as well as a slowly revolving sightseeing deck and a restaurant for tourists, all under a strobe light that could be seen by airline pilots flying over New York City, more than four hundred miles away.

To finance the building of the tower, the banks offered to give us a new consolidated mortgage loan of $16 million on all of our properties except the government-financed Cathedral apartments. This would pay off all our present debts. The banks advanced us $475,000 so we could start construction of the tower while the appraisal of the other properties was being made. After the 560-foot concrete section of the structure was completed, we received a detailed proposal for the financing based on the appraisal. To my astonishment, the plan for the $16 million mortgage loan called for all of our properties—the television production company, which was doing commercial work in addition to our own ministry's video work; the Buffet; our downtown office building; the tower; and the Cathedral of Tomorrow itself—to be incorporated into a single real estate trust.

I could never agree. Our church could not be included in such a trust with our commercial properties. It would violate my promise to God never to use our church for commercial purposes. Furthermore, I did not own the Cathedral of Tomorrow building; it officially belonged to the members of our congregation. I was only one of the members of the board of trustees who managed the church for the congregation. If our people learned that I had put up their church as security to raise money for the tower we were planning—a commercial project with a commercial TV studio and transmitter, a restaurant, and a sightseeing deck for tourists—I would have been fired and run out of town...and should have been!

The bankers now refused to give us a consolidated mortgage unless the church was included in the trust. So the deal fell through, and the tower remained unfinished.

I began to wonder why God had allowed us to build the main structure of the tower then suddenly stopped the construction before we could put the restaurant and transmitter on its top. Was God telling me something? Did He want the tower to stand for a higher purpose than an attraction for tourists?

Why, in fact, were we becoming involved in a commercial TV business? We had established our church to bring the Gospel to people all over the world through television. Operating a commercial television station and selling advertising were quite another matter. Even though the profits from our proposed ultrahigh-frequency TV channel would be used to support God's work, maybe the time and energy we would devote to such a project would detract from our ability to carry on the very work it was supposed to support, the work for God in our church and television ministry.

Every time I parked my car beside the Cathedral and looked up at the unfinished tower, I thought about the message God was plainly trying to give me. I began to wonder about our involvement in other uncompleted enterprises: Cathedral Tele-Productions, our leased office building in downtown Akron, Mackinac College. Were these costly diversions distracting too

155

much of my attention from the work of spreading the Gospel that God had called me to do? Were they the modern-day equivalent of my father's orphanage—worthwhile, but wrong for the ministry in other ways?

God soon gave the answer to these questions, loud and clear.

THE CRASH

Our TV audience was growing every week. We had received 690,000 letters from viewers in 1970; now, two years later, the volume had doubled. A staff of ten counselors in our Cathedral Prayer Group worked around the clock taking calls from people in spiritual need all over the country and praying with them for God to intervene. We were supporting missionaries all over the world. All of my dreams were coming true!

And then came the crash.

I had felt drawn to Europe for evangelism, so in December 1972 Maude Aimee and I took a combined business trip and vacation. We arranged a series of revivals in Sweden for the following summer and investigated the possibility of putting our programs on the air in England, France, and elsewhere on the continent. As Maude Aimee and I flew home from London, we were looking forward to spending the merriest Christmas ever with our children and grandchildren.

Instead, we came home to a firestorm of newspaper headlines: court actions had been brought against us by federal and state government authorities; they were threatening to take the Cathedral of Tomorrow away from us and shut down our television broadcasting.

Reeling, I tried to piece together what had happened…and what was about to happen.

On Abraham Lincoln's birthday, February 12, 1973, the U.S. Securities and Exchange Commission (SEC) and the Ohio Commerce Department brought actions against the Cathedral of Tomorrow, effectively forcing us into receivership—bankruptcy—on charges of illegal fund raising. The big headlines in the newspapers sounded as if our church was about to be closed down because Rex Humbard had defrauded the bond and note holders who had invested their money in the ministry. You had to read down into the small print at the bottom of the page before you found out that the officials were saying I had been honest in my dealings with our investors, that I had never cheated anybody out of a single cent, and that we had always made all of our interest payments on time. Furthermore, as the Ohio director of commerce told reporters, "Anybody who wanted to get his investment back has always been able to do so."

The shocking charges against us and the threat of receivership were based on what amounted to a technicality: the authorities claimed we had violated security laws because we borrowed funds without issuing to our bond and note holders a detailed financial statement of our church's debts, liabilities, and assets. It was an astounding charge because we had never tried to hide our heavy debts. It had never occurred to us or our lawyers that it was illegal for our church to borrow money from members of our congregation without giving them a financial statement, because other churches had been doing it for years. In fact, many still do it to this day. Our investors weren't putting their money into a business venture; they were helping us share the Gospel of Jesus Christ. None of them ever even *requested* a financial statement!

"It's the devil trying to stop us," Maude Aimee said to me with tears in her eyes. "How come we're the only church having this trouble? The devil is mad at us because we've been doing so well, that's why!"

I had to agree, and the authorities appeared to have a similar perspective. Why had one independent Christian church in Cuyahoga Falls, Ohio, been singled out for prosecution on a charge that could have been leveled against hundreds, if not thousands, of other churches across the

157

country? Perhaps because our televised evangelistic programs were attracting more people every Sunday than all of the combined congregations of all the denominational churches?

Our entire operation screeched to a halt. We were forced to stop raising money by selling bonds and interest-bearing notes. I offered the government a plan to pay back our investors with the $14 million that would be coming to us from wills and annuities within a few years. They refused. I felt like a man with a mortgage on his family's home who expects to pay it off in monthly installments over the next seven years, but who suddenly gets a message from the bank that if he doesn't pay the entire loan next week, he will lose the house.

On the face of it, there appeared to be three courses of action open to us. First, we could go into bankruptcy, but I couldn't even think of such a thing. If we went into bankruptcy, none of our bond and note holders, who had lent us more than $12.5 million over several years, would ever be repaid, and the mortgages on our church and its properties would be foreclosed.

Secondly, we could go to court and fight the SEC and state securities regulators, charging that their interference in our church's financial affairs was a violation of our First Amendment safeguards of religious freedom. In such a legal contest, the federal and state authorities would have asked for our church to be put into receivership, with a court-appointed receiver controlling our management during the course of the case. We would have lost control of our church and our television ministry. Our dream of spreading the Gospel all over the world would have been demolished then and there.

The third course open to us offered our one and only slim hope of survival.

We would have to ask God for a miracle.

EIGHT

Desperation and Deliverance

 $\mathcal{W}$ e decided to offer to put our church's financial affairs under court scrutiny—not under formal receivership—while we cleared up all of our heavy debts immediately. First, we would cut expenses to the bone and stop all deficit spending. In plain English, deficit spending meant putting money into enterprises that were in the red financially. In our case, this included Mackinac College, Cathedral Tele-Productions, and our downtown office building. Our deficit spending was at an all-time high of $5.4 million a year at the time; it was a cancer that had to be cut out immediately.

Then, with our expenses cut down, we could take on the really hard part of our survival plan. We would ask the court for time to raise a trust fund of several million dollars. This extra money would have to come from special gifts given by our church members and people in our television audience. We couldn't borrow it because we couldn't take on new debts. When we had enough money in this trust fund, we would offer it for payback of any bond and note holders who wanted their money immediately. This would give our bond and note program a clean bill of legal health. The federal and state authorities would withdraw their action against our church. We would be free once again to go on with the great work of taking the message of Jesus Christ to all people all over the world through television.

It was a plan of desperation, and we had only a narrow chance of being able to carry it out. Rex Junior and I argued with our lawyers and advisers, who doubted we would ever be able to raise such a three or four million dollar trust fund. How could we put aside that much money, they asked, while we were paying all our monthly expenses and keeping all our television programs on the air at the same time?

But this was the very thing I was determined to do. I was willing to do anything to keep our church out of receivership or bankruptcy so we would not be forced to black out a single one of the television stations carrying our programs anywhere in the United States or Canada.

"We'll do it by praying for God's help," I said. "He'll see us through this trouble. God has never let us down, and He won't let us down this time."

Finally, in May of 1973, the SEC and the Department of Commerce agreed. In the two months leading up to this decision, we made sweeping cuts in our expenses. On March 1, a sad day at the Cathedral, we reduced our payroll by two hundred staffers, many of whom had worked with us faithfully for many years. We sold the Brooklyn girdle company and the small printing and advertising agency which had been publishing our monthly *Answer* magazine as well as our booklets and pamphlets. We closed Mackinac College, saving $140,000 a year. We turned the lease on our downtown office building back over to John W. Galbreath, who had donated it to us. We had expected to earn a profit of $150,000 a year on that building and to pour that money into Mackinac College. But it was not to be; it would take too long to generate the profits.

We also closed Cathedral Tele-Productions, even though it was on the verge of becoming a highly profitable commercial enterprise that would soon provide income for the overseas expansion of our television ministry. We had made a big investment in color video equipment in 1968, then used that equipment to produce commercials and educational and documentary videos for various television production companies. Now all of that was over.

When our financial crisis forced us to stop deficit spending, I realized that God was giving me the answer I'd been seeking since He had stopped construction of our tower-top TV station. In my eagerness to expand our television ministry, I had gotten us too involved in commercial business enterprises. As I talked over our situation with Maude Aimee, Rex Junior, and Don, we agreed that we should give up *all* of our commercial projects. From that point on, we promised ourselves, we would limit our work to the service of God. Instead of trying to supplement our church's offerings and donations with outside business ventures, we would trust in God to provide for His work.

"God, You've got a problem," I prayed. "I'm in sales, not in management. I'm letting You take care of making ends meet from here on in."

BLESSING IN DISGUISE

The crisis was a blessing in disguise. Being forced to cut expenses, to stop borrowing, to pay our debts, we focused our energies and resources like a laser on the one thing to which God had called us. I woke up each morning with a deeper and stronger dedication to God's work. I felt like a fellow who had gone through a lot of pain in the hospital, having a bunch of kidney stones removed; once the stones were gone, he felt a lot better about his future!

But now we faced the second and more difficult part of our survival

161

plan: raising enough money from our loyal friends to pay off any of our bond and note holders who wanted their money back immediately instead of waiting till their loans were actually due. I felt that most of the people who had lent us money to help us preach the Gospel on television would be willing to wait a few more years until the agreed due date. But we estimated that requests for immediate repayment might still come to around $4 million, about one-third the total amount outstanding.

The court agreed to give us six months, until the following November, to raise a $4 million trust fund. If we succeeded by November 1, remaining debt free and continuing to meet our monthly expenses while we raised the money, we could then send all of our bond and note holders a formal offer of repayment. The lawyers called it an offer of "rescission." Any bond or note holder who wanted to be repaid immediately would have two months, till January 3, 1974, to send us a request for repayment.

Trying to raise $4 million in less than six months was difficult enough, but we were under severe legal restrictions that made the task even more difficult. The court ordered me not to discuss full details of our financial emergency before our congregation in the Cathedral or on our television programs. I couldn't talk about our case to newspaper or TV news reporters. I was also forbidden to communicate personally with any of our bond and note holders. This was a legal precaution to keep me from influencing any of our investors into not asking for their money until it was due.

It's mighty hard to ask people to help you when you can't tell them why you need their help. All I was allowed to say in my appeals on television and in letters to our contributors was that I needed their help immediately to keep our services on television.

On the other hand, however, the federal and state authorities who were prosecuting us had talked freely to newspapers about our case. Even before the court actions were filed against us, there were headlines all over the country about Rex Humbard's financial troubles, about the $12,528,000 that the Cathedral of Tomorrow owed to its bond and note holders, and about our debts and deficit spending. This publicity frightened many bond and note holders into asking for their loans to be repaid immediately, especially the ones who had lent us money as an investment rather than to help us spread the Gospel.

Yet those same headlines told our television audiences what I was unable to tell them: why we were in trouble and why we needed their help. There were millions of people all over the United States and Canada who had been watching our services on TV every Sunday for many years without ever bothering to mail a donation. They had assumed that a church as big and as handsome as the one they were seeing on their television screen must be rolling in money. Now they learned from their newspapers—not from me, because I never talked about our troubles from the pulpit—that our church was broke because we had been begging and borrowing money to expand our television network all over North America and into foreign countries instead of playing it safe and paying off the mortgage.

Those wonderful strangers joined our many loyal friends in sending us generous contributions and messages of encouragement. We began to hear from thousands of people who had never written to us before: Catholic priests and nuns, Protestant ministers and bishops, many people who said they never went to any church but watched us regularly on television, wealthy businessmen, political leaders, poor farmers, laborers. Housewives sent us money they had been saving for a new sewing machine or baby carriage.

Shirley DuBro wrote on behalf of herself and her husband, Art:

If we had not turned on our TV one Sunday and just happened to hear you, we might still be searching for the truth. Once we found your program

163

and your message, we started sending your ministry a little money each month, usually around $20. We had no large bank account. Sometimes on Sunday when we would sit down to write your check, it would leave nothing in our account. But when we read in our paper of your trouble, our hearts were troubled deeply. My husband came to me and said, "We'll have to help Rex. I'm sending him $100, and from here on, we'll send him 10% of our income, whatever it is." It frightened me, because I knew how slim our bank account was, and how big our debts, but I said, "Go ahead. God will supply our needs." Well, since then there has not been a single week that we have not been able to send between $50 and $100 per week, not per month. We have doubled our business income. There has never been a time, after we sent your check on Sunday, that God does not "throw it back into the nest"—and more, usually by the end of the next day.

Shirley's letter was remarkably typical. The newspaper stories about our predicament, which damaged our reputation among many people, brought us help from many others.

Then came another tragedy.

RUIN AND REDEMPTION

The phone rang in our home one Friday night. It was terrible news. The kitchen of our Cathedral Buffet had been completely destroyed by fire. The news struck me so hard, coming on top of all our other heartaches, that Maude Aimee thought I was having a heart attack. I almost thought so myself.

"Are you trying to outdo Job in the Bible?" a friend asked me the next day, and by then I was able to smile a bit in response. Indeed, I did seem to be imitating that unhappy man in the Old Testament whose faith was tested by so many trials and misfortunes. When we looked at the Buffet's damage, however, we said a prayer of thanks, because the fire had been contained inside the kitchen, without destroying the restaurant's elaborately decorated dining room or spreading to our expensively equipped video facilities in the same building.

And on the following Sunday morning, I was surprised to see one of the Buffet hostesses coming forward to answer my altar call at the end of our service in the Cathedral. She had been our friend for many years, a waitress in a restaurant where we took our children in our early days in Akron, long before she joined our Buffet staff. Suddenly, as she walked down the aisle that Sunday morning, I realized that I had never seen her in church before. But this was understandable since Sunday was her busiest day of work at the Buffet, where we often served Sunday dinner to more than thirty-eight hundred people.

Then it dawned on me: this good woman would never have been able to attend our church on this particular Sunday, when she discovered faith in Jesus Christ and came forward to pray for His forgiveness, had the Buffet not been closed because of the fire! If that fire was responsible for bringing just one soul to God, it was well worth all the trouble it caused.

* * *

As it turned out, the Buffet had to be closed for several months. We told ourselves that things had to get better because they couldn't get any worse. And indeed, God provided for us once again, as always.

Despite the legal restrictions that blurred my appeals for help, we received enough contributions in the seven-month period before November 1 to put $3.5 million into the trust fund, while we paid off other debts and running expenses—and never missed a single payment on our big weekly television bills. Our financial advisers and the court and government securities officials who were watching our business affairs were all astonished by this performance.

Then the trustees of Jimmy Hoffa's Teamsters Union pension fund came to our aid, as they had in the past. They had already agreed to suspend payments on the principal of their mortgage until we cleared up our debts and got ourselves released from the court's supervision, but now the pension fund's trustees gave us a loan for $500,000, increasing their mortgage by that amount and enabling us to add the amount to our trust fund.

This pushed our drive over the top. Now we had the whole $4 million to cover the estimated cost of repaying the bond and note holders who were expected to ask for their money back before the January 3 deadline.

Maude Aimee and I thanked God for lifting a great weight of worry from our hearts. We had gone through the most difficult crisis of our lives.

Unfortunately, it wasn't over.

ANOTHER DARK SKY

It was an ironic Christmas. The year before, we had struggled through the Christmas season with the terrible shock of the government actions against our ministry. This year we were looking forward to our merriest Christmas ever. Ahead of us was a new year which promised to be our greatest ever. We were free from debt. We would be free from the court's supervision. Our church was already in the black financially for the first time since we opened its doors back in 1953.

But then came January. The repayments requested by bond and note holders were totaled up, and their demands added up to $8.3 million, more than twice the amount we had expected to pay.

I was stunned. We had struggled for a year to get out of trouble. Now, when we were just beginning to see some light, the sky had suddenly darkened again.

Heartsick, we mailed to the bond and note holders checks for 49 percent of the amount owed them. Now we had to raise the other 51 percent, another $4.3 million. We could never expand our television ministry all over the world while we had this enormous debt hanging over our heads and the state authorities supervising our spending.

I surveyed the landscape of our ministry. During the past year of expense cutting and retrenchment, we had managed to hold on to every one of our television stations in North America. But we had been forced to stop our overseas broadcasts, which we had started very successfully in Australia, the Philippines, and Japan in the fall of 1972. I wanted to put the Cathedral of Tomorrow back on television overseas as soon as possible, not five or six years from now.

I also realized that the longer we remained in debt, the sooner we would be forced to make further cuts in expenses—and this time those cuts would have to be made in our North American television coverage, the only frontier we had left. Our financial watchdogs knew that our church could easily save a few hundred thousand dollars a month simply by dropping a few of our TV channels here and there in the United States and Canada.

This was a backward step I refused to take. We had worked too hard for over twenty years, putting God on television coast-to-coast, to allow even a single one of our 360 TV channels to be blacked out.

So we had to raise $4.3 million immediately and pay off the rest of the money owed to bond and note holders, not during the next year, not during the next six months, but immediately. Right now.

We didn't know any wealthy angel or any charitable foundation likely to give us that much money. There was only one way to get it.

We would have to pray for it.

ASKING FOR A MIRACLE

On Sunday, February 17, 1974, I asked the members of our Prayer Key Family and the millions of other people watching us on television all across the continent to fast and pray with me during the coming week for God to give us that miracle.

I fasted that entire week. Many of our people at the Cathedral fasted along with me. We began to see signs that God was answering our prayers, but I didn't stop fasting. Instead, I prayed all the harder and kept on fasting for two more weeks, drinking a little water or a cup of tea or coffee now and then, but never eating any solid food. Fasting for such a miracle as this was no big hardship for me. I actually never felt better than I did during those three weeks of "sacrifice," giving up my daily bread for the greater glory of the Lord.

One day during the second week of my fast, I drove downtown to keep a lunchtime appointment in a restaurant with a friend who had some business matters to discuss with me. He was familiar with my work and our current financial problems, but he wasn't a member of our church and not a deeply religious-minded person. When I asked our server to bring me just a cup of tea, my companion looked at me with dismay.

"Rex, why do you keep punishing yourself?" he asked. "I don't mean just this fasting, although that's bad enough. I mean why do you go on breaking your back and getting into financial trouble because you're trying to put your Bible preaching and praying on television all over America and the whole world? You could have stopped expanding ten years ago, when you had fifty stations here in the Midwest. Then you would have had a big audience every Sunday and no more money troubles. Why go on and on, trying to reach more and more people?"

I could only quote the words of Christ from Mark 16:15: "Go into all

168

the world, and preach the gospel to every creature." I pointed out to my friend that God didn't say to go into a few states in the Midwestern part of the U.S. and preach to as many people as we can afford to reach without borrowing money. He said to preach to *every* creature *everywhere.*

"But God didn't say to preach on television," my friend said. "I've always thought that a minister had to preach in a church. Don't people have to go to a church in order to learn how to believe in God, and isn't a church the only place where a person can pray?"

I explained to my friend, as I have often explained to many other people, that too many of us have been conditioned to think that a church has to be a building with a steeple, a pulpit, and an altar, a meetinghouse with pews and ushers to show you to your seat. There's not a single sentence in the Bible that says we have to worship God in such a building. In fact, the New Testament tells us that Jesus avoided the temples and houses of worship where the elders and Pharisees didn't want to listen to Him. He did His preaching along the highways and byways, in the city streets and the country lanes. The Bible makes it plain that Jesus did His work anywhere and everywhere. When a man asked Jesus to come to his home to cure his sick son, Jesus replied, "Go your way; your son lives" (John 4:50). There's no need for God to work in a particular place or in a particular setting or atmosphere. Receiving God's message is the important thing, not where or how you receive it.

A farmer in North Dakota who prayed devoutly in front of his television screen when he heard me in the Cathedral of Tomorrow at Cuyahoga Falls, Ohio, certainly is as close to God as the people who prayed with me inside our church building. There are too many of us who believe that you can't pray effectively unless you're kneeling in a church; there are also too many Christians who think you can't be saved unless you attend their particular church and accept its ritual, doctrine, and interpretation of the Bible.

We met with disapproval from traditionalists from the beginning. But I soon saw that television in the mid- to late-twentieth century had exactly the power that I sensed it would have: the power to attract the previously disinterested, even the skeptically prejudiced. I could fill a book with the stories of people who let us know that they first tuned in to our Cathedral of Tomorrow broadcasts only by chance or accident. They had no intention or desire to find a religious program that day. But then they stayed, they prayed, and they found peace and joy. Some told us they found our program only because it was raining too hard for a long-planned family picnic, or because the movie on another channel was too blurry, or because an alcoholic hangover kept them from sleeping.

In one brief letter from Cleveland, a viewer told us that he had been a criminal for many years, involved in the drug trade and other kinds of organized crime. Without giving any details, he said that after watching our Sunday services on television, he and his wife had accepted Christ and that he had now given up his life of crime. Wayne and I couldn't resist visiting to find out more.

He had been in and out of prison since his teens, he told us, and deeply involved in organized crime.

"I turned your program on one Sunday morning when I had a bad hangover," he told me rather sheepishly. "I was a terrible drinker. This particular Sunday I woke up feeling bad and took a couple of drinks, and I decided to turn on the TV, and there you were. You'd say something, and I'd take another drink and cuss you out and curse you and tell you that you were full of bull. I felt mean, and I enjoyed cussing you and telling you off. The next Sunday I woke up and said to my wife, 'I wonder if that guy's on again.' I turned you on, and listened, and when you said something, I'd cuss at you and take another drink. That went on every Sunday morning for several weeks. It got to be a habit. You'd say something, and I would cuss at you."

Finally one Sunday his wife complained that he was being disrespectful, swearing so much in the presence of a preacher of the Gospel. "The
next thing I knew," he said, "we were agreeing not to drink while you
were on the air. Then we had a talk and decided that if drinking and cursing in front of you was disrespectful, it must be disrespectful to the good
Lord above. Then when you were praying one Sunday we knelt down in
the front of the TV screen and prayed along with you. We both quit
drinking. I went to the guys in the mob and told them I was leaving them
and going straight from now on. They threatened to kill me, but they
haven't hit me yet, so maybe they won't. I got a legitimate job, and we
started going to church."

"We are happy," his wife said, "for the first time in our lives."

Television made the difference for them! It set them on the road to
freedom.

I long ago lost count of the numbers of divorced couples who have
asked me to remarry them because their spiritual values were awakened
through our television programs, and they came to a new and stronger
love for and understanding of each other. One couple suffered such a bit-
ter divorce that the husband turned his back on his family and didn't even
ask for permission to visit his children for more than three years. He had
been living near Columbus, in the center of Ohio, and his wife, never
hearing a word from him, established a home for herself and their children
at Ashtabula in the northeast corner of the state, 160 miles away. One
Sunday morning her telephone rang, and she was surprised to hear the
voice of her ex-husband speaking to her for the first time in three years.

"There's a show on television I'd like you to look at," he said.

"What show is that?"

"It's called the *Cathedral of Tomorrow*, with a preacher called Rex
Humbard."

"I watch it every week," she replied. "I've got it on the TV right now."

171

"I've been watching it too," the man said, "and it's got me thinking about something. When we were living together, we never went to church and we never took our kids to church. Maybe if we had gone to church, we wouldn't have gotten the divorce."

"Maybe you're right," the woman replied.

"Why don't we go to Akron sometime and go to church at this Cathedral of Tomorrow?" he said.

"Well, why don't you come up here some Sunday," she answered, "and we'll do that?"

"How about next Sunday?"

The next Sunday morning the man got up at 4:00 a.m., drove 160 miles to Ashtabula, picked up his ex-wife and their four children, turned around and drove another 80 miles to the Cathedral of Tomorrow. At the conclusion of that day's services, when I invited people to join me in a prayer of repentance for salvation, those two parents and their four children came forward. Later, when we invited them into a private room for counseling, they told us that they had decided to make another try at their marriage.

On another Sunday morning, a few weeks later, they returned to the Cathedral with a marriage license. I asked them if they would stand up before the congregation and tell how they had been separated, without going into the specific details of the disagreement, and how they had been reconciled through their new faith in Christ. They said they would be proud to do it. When I presented them to the congregation, I joked with the woman: "What's that you've got there in your hand?"

"That's our marriage license," she replied. "We want to be married again."

I called their children up. They ran down the aisle and scrambled up onto the stage. I got out my marriage book and remarried them right then and there. The last we heard from them, they were still as happy as could be.

There were countless thousands of other stories like theirs, each with its own twist. But in every case, the initial attraction to the Gospel came *not* from the preacher—I'm not that magnetic!—but from God. I saw God at work through this evangelism strategy. It was the testimony of so many TV-attracted converts that made me so deeply dedicated to the work of expanding our television evangelism effort all over North America and into foreign countries, even though such expansion plunged us deeply and dangerously into debt.

And it was the memory of those conversions to Christ that encouraged me to ask God for the miracle that would keep our ministry alive and let it grow again.

And it was the memory of those conversions to Christ that encouraged me to ask God for the miracle that would keep our ministry alive and let it grow again.

On a Tavern Floor

Television, in a way, is a one-way street. Back at the Cathedral of Tomorrow or in our studios, we had no way of seeing the men and women of Seattle, Fort Worth, Toronto, or Worcester who were kneeling to pray in front of their TV screens when I invited them to ask God for His forgiveness. Perhaps we heard about 1 percent of the unseen conversions, through letters, phone calls, or chance meetings with converts at our rallies. At one rally in Boise, Idaho, the local Baptist minister introduced us to a married couple who told me that during the first eight years of their marriage, neither of them had given a thought to the existence of God. Then one Sunday morning when their three children were still asleep in bed upstairs, they happened to see our program on television for the first time. The videotaped broadcast of our services was then shown in Boise at an early hour, from 8:00 to 9:00 a.m. After listening to my sermon and hearing my invitation to pray, the husband and wife knelt down before their TV screen and asked for God's forgiveness. Then they went upstairs, woke their children, got them dressed, and took them to the nearby Baptist church to attend the 11:00 a.m. service. The family has been attending church regularly ever since!

After another rally in Michigan, a woman told me that she had been deeply depressed, on the verge of suicide, until she heard Maude Aimee and Leona singing "Reach Out to Jesus" on our TV program.

"Right then and there," the woman told me, "I reached out to Jesus. I dedicated my life to Him, and now I find it a joy to be alive."

Down through the years we also heard bits and pieces of unfinished stories about needy souls grasping for the peace that passes understanding (Philippians 4:7) that they'd heard about on our shows. I received a sad note in the mail, scribbled on a scrap of paper—the back of a package that had contained a painkilling drug—found on the floor of a Milwaukee tavern.

"Dear God," it began, "please have Mr. Hummbard pray for me. Please, I sure need it, and I've forgotten how. He won't know who or where this came from, but You will."

There was no signature.

The man who sent me the scrap of paper enclosed a note himself: "Dear Rex: It's not a habit of mine to pick up scraps of paper from tavern floors. But I did pick up this one, and now I know why. How else could it have been delivered to you if God didn't see to it? So now I am forwarding it to you. Incidentally, Mr. Humbard, I know how to spell your name. I watch your program."

I have prayed often for that poor anonymous soul. One Sunday I asked our congregation at the Cathedral and our television audience to pray for him. I often wonder what happened to him. If he had faith enough to write that note, I have to believe he's winning his battle, by the grace of God!

"Ask, and You Shall Receive"

The ministry of our twenty-four-hour Prayer Group alone would have been enough to pray and fast and work and sweat and fight for. At its peak, our prayer team received six thousand calls in a single month, in addition to thousands of letters, literally from around the world. Our Prayer Group prayed for people dealing with every conceivable type of problem: from broken arms to broken marriages, from anger to addiction, from trouble with the law to trouble with money. And we saw God answer prayer again and again.

One woman told us that she was stricken with severe pain late at night when she was alone in her home. Her husband was away, and her only child, a twelve-year-old daughter, was visiting a cousin in another town. The woman's telephone was out of order, so it was impossible for her to call anyone for help. Moreover, the hour was so late that all of the other houses in her neighborhood were locked and in darkness. So the woman scraped together as much change as she could find in her pocketbook and piggy bank, and made her way down the street to an outdoor pay phone near a closed gas station. From there she called our Prayer Group. While the counselor was praying for her, the pain left her body instantly. She was able to go home and sleep peacefully.

Over the years we received reports of averted suicides, healed marriages, resolved work problems, and the list goes on. In addition to phone requests, our Prayer Group prayed over many more thousands of prayer requests sent by mail. Thousands of letters also came from people reporting how prayer had changed their lives. They had learned from personal experience that God answers prayer! The same phrases were repeated in their letters: "My husband tells me that I have a peace of mind that I never had before," "A great load of worry has been lifted from me because I no longer fear death," and on and on!

I have always taught that prayer is not something to turn to only after everything else has failed. Pray now, today and every day, for things you need to make your life happy and enjoyable. The Bible says in John 16:24, "Ask, and you will receive that your joy may be full." It doesn't say "Ask only when you are in desperate need." Ungodly and worldly people get what they want by scheming, struggling, fighting, and waging wars for it. Godly Christian people get what they want by praying and asking God for it. The Bible also says in James 4:2, "You do not have because you do not ask." It is as simple as that!

But in the best of times and in the worst of times, whether you are merely asking for a youngster to pass a high school physics exam, or your mother is facing serious surgery, sincere and heartfelt prayer works. God pays just as much attention to requests for small favors as He does to desperate pleas for help in big emergencies. I am grateful that no job is too big or too small for God.

A viewer wrote from Asheville, North Carolina:

I am writing a letter of thanksgiving. It has been two years since I accidentally turned on your program.... I was then an invalid and had been sent home to die by the doctors in the hospital. I had been ill for almost seven years, and during that time I had my leg amputated. I had bleeding ulcers...they could not operate.... I had to have narcotics around the clock for over four and a half years. The doctor said I would never be able to get off drugs. I weighed less than a hundred pounds.

I listened to your program and it stirred my soul to the point that it gave me a ray of hope, even though I had prayed constantly to God to take me home. I asked my wife to write to you and request prayer. After about three weeks of listening to your preaching, she noticed that I had been taking less medication than before. Each time you had your anointing service I would bow down before the television set and pray with you.

At the end of six weeks I went to the doctor, and he gave me a clean bill of health. Your prayers gave me the hope I needed and God performed a miracle. I have been working now for a year at the university. I want the whole world to know what God has done for me.

Letters like this strengthened my deep conviction that prayer is the most powerful force in the universe and inspired me to organize the alliance of dedicated Christians pledging themselves to pray together every Sunday while watching our television program: our Prayer Key Family.

And it was because of the power of prayer, which I had witnessed so many times through the years, that I turned to our Prayer Key Family in our hour of deepest need. When we needed a miracle to keep our ministry alive, I asked our television family to come together, go to God, and intercede for the sake of our television ministry.

THE LEPERS' DEBATE

I wish I had some way of knowing just how many men, women, boys, and girls all over North America answered my call for help during that "Miracle Week" in February of 1974. I am sure that never before in the history of the Christian church had there been so many prayers and so much fasting and giving by so many millions of people at the same time—all of them asking God for the same blessing: the saving of the Cathedral of Tomorrow's worldwide television ministry.

Technically speaking, my appeal for help may have been illegal. As I

prepared for that sermon, knowing it would be literally the most important of my life, I made up my mind to explain fully and openly just
exactly why our need was so urgent. For the entire previous year, I had
strictly obeyed the court order not to discuss the details of my troubles
with my church's congregation or on our television broadcasts. I'm sure if
I had been allowed to explain exactly why we needed help, we could have
wiped all of our debts off the books in short order. Pat Boone and other
friends pleaded with me at that time to let *them* go on the air and explain
to the public my need for help. But I asked them to remain silent, in
accordance with the court's restrictions.

Now, needing $4.3 million to close the gap on the demands of bond
and note holders for immediate payment, I told myself that this was the
time to defy the court. I would open my heart and tell the world why I
needed help.

I opened my sermon that day, on February 17, with the story of the
lepers in 2 Kings 7 who were sitting beside the gate of Samaria when the
city was surrounded by an army of its enemies, its food and water supply
cut off. The people inside the city were starving. The lepers were debat-
ing what they should do.

"If we go back into the city, we'll starve to death," one of them said.
"If we sit here by the gate where we usually beg for alms and food, we'll
die. Why sit here and die? Let's go out and face the army of the enemies.
Maybe they'll kill us, but if we stay here we'll die anyway; and if they
don't kill us, maybe they'll have mercy on us and give us food."

So the lepers staggered out to face the army. God saw their faith, and
made their footsteps sound like thunder. The enemies thought the thun-
dering noise was a rival army coming to save Samaria. The soldiers panicked and ran away, leaving all of their food and supplies behind them.
The lepers found the plentiful food, and hurried back into the city to tell
the Samarians that they had been saved by God.

Then I compared our situation with that of the lepers of Samaria. "Twenty-one years ago," I said, "we stayed in Akron with sixty-five dollars to start a church that would someday bring its Sunday services and the message of Jesus Christ by television to people all over the United States and Canada, and then all over the world. Now that television ministry is facing a challenge. What are we going to do? We're not going to sit here and die. We're going to go out and meet that challenge."

I explained in detail our trouble and our need—how our bond and note program had been questioned legally by the federal and state securities agencies and how we were trying to conform to government regulations by offering to repay in full any bond or note holders who wanted immediate repayment instead of meeting those obligations over the next seven years, as we had planned to do.

"How would you feel," I asked, "if you had a mortgage on your home with a big balance of several thousand dollars, which you were paying off in monthly payments, and suddenly the savings bank said to you, 'Pay up the whole balance today'? You'd be in trouble, wouldn't you? That's what has happened to this ministry."

I told our people how we had struggled to build up a fund to cover the expected repayments and how we had sent out an offer to meet such requests, only to find that our fund could cover less than half of the amount demanded.

"We have mailed checks for forty-nine cents of every dollar requested," I said. "The challenge now is, what do we do about the other 51 percent? We could raise that money by not supporting our missionaries overseas any longer or by stopping the publication of our monthly magazine and our various religious booklets. Or we could take our Sunday programs off television in places like Alberta and Nova Scotia, or Arkansas and Florida. That would give us the money to pay off all of our loans. But is that what God wants us to do?

"I believe God wants us to expect a miracle. Millions of people go to church with us here on television every Sunday. Just as the lepers went out to face the army of the enemy and found plenty of food, not only for themselves but for all the starving people in Samaria, God wants us to have a miracle not only to meet this need but to provide us with plenty more to carry the Gospel around the whole world before Jesus comes again, for these are the last days."

Then I declared that the coming week, February 17–24, would be Miracle Week in the ministry of the Cathedral of Tomorrow. I asked everybody who was listening to me to pray every day that week for the miracle we needed, and to fast on Wednesday, February 20. "I'm going to be fasting all week," I said, "but I want every one of you to fast for at least that one day. And I want a letter from every one of you who believe in this ministry. We're going to meet this challenge. We're not going to sit down and die."

Already Happening

That week, Maude Aimee and I mailed certified letters to everybody who had ever given a contribution to our ministry, asking for help. Pat Boone spent a whole day at his home in California writing a letter to send to people in our television audience, with each copy reproduced on his own stationery in his own handwriting. Pat was concerned about people who might not have received his letter because their address had been changed or because they might have been away from home when it was delivered. So he asked us if he could appear on our television programs on the Sunday after Miracle Week, March 3, to deliver his message personally.

"You always hurt more for one you love than you do for yourself," Pat said. "I have hurt deeply this past year for our dear friend Rex Humbard, whom I love, respect, and admire as few men alive and in Gospel service today.

"Repeatedly this past year I begged Rex to let me tell his side of the story. I was filled with righteous indignation that this great ministry for Jesus was being blatantly misrepresented through the news media, without the full story being disclosed.

"But, like the faithful shepherd that he is, Rex stood silent in his own defense and continued to preach the Gospel without fear. He stood tall, and I imagine you were as proud of him as I was.

"At last, Rex has sent you a letter himself. I still don't think he's said all he should in his own defense. But that's Rex.

"And I'm not sure he conveyed to you that the battle is almost won. Almost! One last push will do it. This burden is heavy on my heart, as I'm sure it is on yours. We need this worldwide ministry for Christ, and I feel this man has been persecuted. Jesus said this would happen in Matthew 5:10-12 and Matthew 24:3-14. The times are urgent, so let's help Rex when he needs us most…and get the job done!"

As Pat was speaking for our ministry from his generous heart, the battle was indeed almost won. Our miracle was already happening. Many thousands of letters had been coming to the Cathedral of Tomorrow every day for the past two weeks. People who couldn't send us a contribution wrote to tell us that they were praying and fasting for the survival of our ministry. All of us at the Cathedral and our spouses and children pitched in to help with the work of sorting and opening the piles of letters in our mail room from early morning until after midnight—Maude Aimee, our daughter Elizabeth, Wayne and Leona, Rex Jr. and Don and their wives, the Kokers, the Cathedral Singers, our choir members, our TV cameramen, our Sunday school teachers, Prayer Group counselors, and other volunteers from our local congregation!

There was one letter from a ten-year-old boy with twenty-five pennies glued to a sheet of paper—and twenty-two cents postage due, which we gladly paid. There was a letter from a man in Florida who had never written to us before: "Dear Rex: Here is a check for $2,000, and if you need more let me know." Another man wrote, "I wrote this letter, asking for your prayers, and sealed it before listening to your Sunday program today. Now I am reopening it to put into it this $1,100 that I was saving for a new car. I do this because you have asked, and Christ said if any man asks you to take him a mile, take him two miles."

Four children on a farm in South Dakota sent us their savings: more than eighteen dollars in coins. "You are our pastor," they wrote, "and we like you. We want to help. We are praying." Then they added a P.S.: "Daddy is going to sell two calves tomorrow and he will wire you the money." A woman enclosed a note with her contribution that said, "Every year on my birthday my husband sends me roses. I asked him not to this year so we could send this gift to you. Roses fade. Christ's work must not."

A man in New Orleans wrote: "I was driving to work, wishing that I could send you $100, and then I said to myself, I will play some numbers at the races. Well, I hit one of the numbers so I am sending you the $100 to help you. You can see how true it is that the Lord will always open a door. I give the Lord all the thanks for helping me to help you."

A psychiatrist wrote: "My profession brings me in contact with many depressed people. Many of them have told me that your television ministry is what 'keeps them going.' I am enclosing a small donation to help you maintain a program that so many people have found to be very helpful."

I received donations and letters of encouragement from Protestant ministers of various denominations and from Catholic priests. "I believe in your ministry," one priest wrote. "I think you are saving many souls as an instrument of God Himself." Maude Aimee's brother, the Rev. Charles Jones, and his wife, Aretes, sent us a thousand dollars which had been contributed by their congregation, Bethel Temple in Fort Worth, Texas. The pastor of two small Methodist churches in North Carolina sent us an offering from his members. "We have been richly blessed by your services," the minister wrote, "which come to us here every Sunday morning before we conduct our own church meetings. This morning you told us how people were suddenly demanding payments of loans. God impressed me to take your plight to my people, and their response was a real joy to see. We just don't want to lose your program here or in any part of the world. God is certainly using you and your people in a marvelous way. Keep up the great work."

A young married couple in Texas had saved their money for a long time to join the party of tourists who were planning to travel with me to Jerusalem during the coming Easter season. They decided to cancel their eagerly awaited trip to the Holy Land so they could get their money refunded and give it instead to our emergency fund.

Another contribution came from a seventy-eight-year-old woman in Indiana. "This is the first letter I have ever written to you," she said, "but we went to your meetings in the tent at Evansville, Indiana, and Owensboro, Kentucky, when your dad was doing the preaching, and Maude Aimee and you were a young couple. I remember your sister, Leona, playing the accordion and her husband strumming that large bass fiddle. All of you have come a long way since then and God has blessed you. We see you and hear you every Sunday because we are shut-ins, married 62 years the 28th of May, and can't go to church. I am sending this $10 to help with your needs and I pray that God will hear your prayers, as I know He will."

Several of the bond and note holders who had asked for repayment and had received checks for 49 percent of the money owed to them in January, wrote to us during Miracle Week in February and told us to keep the rest of their loans. Many other trusting investors who had not requested immediate repayment cashed in their bonds and notes and gave us all the money that we had borrowed from them, saving us many thousands of dollars that we had expected to pay them as interest over the next seven years!

And so God gave us the miracle that we asked for by praying and fasting and giving.

Just three weeks after my initial appeal, I was able to report to our congregation that the miracle had been given to us. We had received not only the rest of the money needed to pay off all the demanded loans but plenty more to help us carry the Gospel on television all over the world. During the previous year we had astonished the government authorities and our own financial managers by raising a fund of $4 million. Now within only three weeks through prayer and sacrifice, we had been given more than $4.5 million!

And the letters were still coming in!

As I told our smiling people on that happy Sunday morning, we were now ready to meet all our obligations. We were going to pay every dime owed to every person who wanted his loan repaid. Every one of our television programs would remain on the air, and every missionary receiving our support would remain at work in the field.

"I serve notice on the devil," I said, "that we are going all over the world to preach the Gospel of Jesus Christ."

A few days later I mailed a letter of thanks to every viewer who had given. "You, my prayer partners, are literally keeping our television ministry alive with your gifts of sacrifice and love. Millions of people, both in the United States and Canada, will someday thank the Lord for your concern for their souls. Thank you again for helping me bring our pulpit into those millions of homes."

I invited them to join me in a special television service on Palm Sunday—a worldwide Communion service—which I would conduct from the Garden Tomb of Christ in Jerusalem, where Jesus arose that first Easter morning. I would carry their names with me to Jerusalem.

"I will lay my hands on your name and pray for you at Calvary," I promised. "Then, by God's miraculous use of television, you and I will take Communion together—you in your home, and I at the open tomb of our Lord."

On that Palm Sunday, I had more reason than ever to rejoice in the power and provision of God. Christ's resurrection, the greatest miracle of all time, was worth celebrating. Yes, and now we could celebrate a new miracle, which would let us take the Good News of that miracle into all the world.

ESKIMOS AND FILIPINOS

A few months later, we were able to add twelve new stations in the United States to our coast-to-coast Sunday television network. We were again preaching the Gospel overseas—in Australia, the Philippines, Japan, Africa, and South America. At the World Congress of Evangelists in Switzerland, I was informed that Eskimos watched our services every Sunday at the Arctic Circle.

Our programs were being beamed to more than 32 million people every week. We had already begun pioneering voiceover dubbing, using electronic sound devices to translate our programs into various foreign languages as the videotape showed us singing and speaking. A translator spoke into a sound track of the video, synchronizing the timing of his words with my own, with other translators playing the voice parts of Maude Aimee and others in our programs. In September 1974 we broadcast our first telecasts in French for audiences in Quebec. What a strange, wonderful sensation to see myself preaching in French instead of Arkansas-accented English! We began dubbing our programs in Japanese, broadcasting on a Tokyo TV station with an audience of more than 3 million. We went all over Latin America in Spanish and all over

Brazil in Portuguese. And along with the foreign-language programs, we translated virtually all of our printed materials into the languages represented by our worldwide audience.

Clearly, God made it possible for us to reach so many souls by giving us the gift of technology—and the faith to pioneer in the uses of it.

NINE

Main Entrance!

$\mathscr{I}$ thought of television—in fact, I thought of many of the "worldly devices," from media to marketing—in terms of the old joke about the three store owners. Their storefronts were side by side, and they sold the same product. One day, the owner on the left put up a sign announcing "30% off." The owner on the right responded by putting up a sign declaring "50% off." The guy in the middle was a little worried until he had a bright idea; he put up a sign over his own door: "Main Entrance— Come This Way!"

I have always been interested in the main entrance. What will interest people? I've spent my life saying "Come this way!" If people were interested in the spectacle of a circus tent, I wanted a circus tent. If they were tuning in to something called radio, I wanted to be on radio. If they were watching TV, I wanted to be there. What's next? Satellite—CD— DVD—Internet. The method doesn't matter. The message, available via the "main door," is what matters. Needy people receiving the message— that's the whole point.

We often made our Cathedral of Tomorrow the main entrance for millions of viewers by featuring celebrity guests. We welcomed the Pittsburgh Steelers' quarterback Terry Bradshaw at the peak of his football career; he sang and shared his testimony. We welcomed Roy Rogers and Dale Evans. We featured Graham Kerr (the "Galloping Gourmet"), Chuck Woolery, Tom Netherton, Corrie ten Boom, Oral and Evelyn Roberts and their son Richard. The first time Pat Boone and his family sang together in public was on the stage of the Cathedral. Our guest list went from Bill Bright to B. J. Thomas. We featured James Cleveland, Norma Zimmer, Jeannie C. Riley, Connie Smith, James Blackwood, the Johnny Mann Singers, George Hamilton IV, Kathy Sullivan—anyone who might connect us to more people in spiritual need.

On one program we welcomed actress Carol Lawrence. She had recently gone through a difficult divorce from Robert Goulet and had been led to faith in Christ through that crisis. As Carol shared what Jesus had done for her, she began to weep. Our cameras moved in so close that you could see a teardrop fall on her dress. Years later I was reviewing videotapes from that era for a restoration project and came across this program. As I sat alone in my office watching Carol's testimony, I began to weep too. In that moment, God confirmed to my spirit the incredible staying power of His anointing. It is not diminished by videotape duplication or by intervening years. His Spirit is still as fresh and real today as the day we taped that program, just as His Word remains as powerful and effective today as it was when it was written thousands of years ago!

The great composer Stuart Hamblin was a frequent guest. He had been a friend for years. Long before we opened the Cathedral, we were recording an album at RCA Studios in Nashville and we needed one more song to complete the project. For a while we were stymied; but then Tim Spencer walked into the studio with a sheet of paper covered with pencil scratchings. "I brought you a song that Stuart just wrote," he said. Tim sat down at the piano and began teaching it to Maude Aimee. The song "Until Then" became a classic. Maude Aimee was the first to record it!

Paths That Cross

The miracles of salvation that God gave us—lost souls saved—could fill a book of their own.

A rough-hewn worker at the Ford plant in Cleveland got into a fight on the job; his hand was so badly injured that he couldn't work for several weeks. Bored, he took a walk with a portable transistor radio in hand. He came across our program, got interested, and kept on walking till he got to our meeting. At the end of that service, he made his way down to the altar, got on his knees, and prayed to accept Christ as Lord and Savior. From that day until his retirement years later, he returned every Sunday morning with one or more of his friends from the Ford plant. Over the years, many of his friends came to faith in Christ. Even in retirement in Florida, this tireless believer faithfully sent us his tithe!

John Seskes was a "motorcycle tough." When he heard me preaching on the radio, he decided to visit the church in order to make fun of me. But God got a hold of his heart that day. "I don't know what happened," he recalled later, "but I went forward and gave my heart to the Lord!" He got into a Bible study, became a serious scholar of the Scriptures, and even ended up on our church staff as our pastor of visitation!

One day I was broadcasting at 10:00 p.m., finished the program, and got in my car. Within a few blocks I came upon an accident scene. A car had hit a concrete post in the median. I stopped and ran to find that the driver had gone completely through the windshield and landed on the street; his clothes were shredded, and there was blood all over him. I didn't touch him. In horror, I knelt down next to him.

"Sir," I asked quietly, "are you alive or dead?"

He opened one eye.

"Aren't you Rex?" he asked.

"Yes, I'm Rex Humbard," I replied.

"I was listening to you on the radio while I was driving," he said.

"Are you a Christian?" I asked.

"I was praying with you on the radio when you prayed," he answered.

"Well, I'm going to pray for you now," I said.

While I was praying, the police came. I finished praying and went on my way.

The next day, the newspaper carried the story of the accident. The man had died.

You never know who will cross your path. You never know what their circumstances are. All you can do is try to help people. Pray for people. Invite people to accept Christ. Connect people to God. That's all I did. That's all I do.

ELVIS

Perhaps the single most famous connection to a soul in need was our extraordinary connection to Elvis Presley.

J. D. Sumner, whose quartet sang backup for Elvis, often slipped into the back of the Cathedral of Tomorrow to enjoy our services. One day he made an unusual request.

"Elvis would sure like to see you and Maude Aimee," he said.

I had heard that Elvis liked our down-to-earth brand of ministry. He called me his "favorite preacher." When he was touring, he sometimes called his staff members to his hotel suite on Sunday mornings to watch our program with him.

Of course we were happy to go. If nothing else, Maude Aimee was a huge fan of Elvis's music! We made arrangements to fly to Las Vegas.

Elvis was at the Hilton. We attended his early show—he was in a double bill—and afterward received an invitation to his dressing room. It was like a television rally of its own, jammed with people. J. D. led us through the crowd, and the moment Elvis saw us, he abandoned everyone else. He led the three of us, including J. D., through the backstage labyrinth and into a little space hardly bigger than a closet. It was so small that we couldn't sit down; we all stood there.

The conversation was amazing to me. Within moments, Elvis was quoting the Bible. He quoted the Old Testament, then the New Testament.

"The Lord's coming soon, isn't he?" Elvis said.

He had a background in the Scriptures. As a boy, he picked his guitar in a Mississippi church. It seemed to me as he talked that he was reaching back into his past.

He spoke of a recent illness he had struggled with. He talked about his mother's recent death. He was discouraged.

Eventually there was an opening, and Maude Aimee spoke up.

"Elvis, you're my bell sheep," she said. "I've been praying for you."

He looked understandably puzzled.

"Over in the Holy Land, they put a bell on the lead sheep," she explained. "As he walks, that bell rings, and all the rest of the sheep follow. I've been praying that you would dedicate your life to Jesus Christ. You'd be my bell sheep, and you could bring thousands, maybe millions, into the kingdom of God."

Elvis went to pieces. He cried so hard that he began to tremble. I took his hands. Maude Aimee did, too. We all joined hands, and I began to pray. I prayed for Elvis for a long time. When I finished, I said, "Elvis, there are other people out here who want to see you. I don't want to take all your time."

"Oh please," he said, "please don't leave."

At that moment the door opened. His little girl, Lisa Marie, came in. "Why is my daddy crying?" she wanted to know.

He patted her on the top of her head.

"It's all right, honey," he said, "I'll be out in a minute."

We kept on talking.

"Elvis, every Christmas, I go to the Holy Land," I told him. "I take letters with me...from people with loved ones who are unsaved, people who have needs. I take these letters and stand at Calvary and I say, 'Lord, by faith I have brought these loved ones' names here. You died for them on the cross here, and I've brought them as an act of faith, to ask you to save them.'"

Elvis was stunned. "How many letters do you take?"

"Last year, we had trunk after trunk full," I said. "Two million, six hundred thousand names, from all over the world: Europe, Asia, North and South America, Africa. We opened them all up, I reached in for a bundle, and they were all in Japanese. I started crying. 'Lord,' I prayed, 'it doesn't make any difference whether I can read them or not, because You know each one of these people, and You're the only one who can do this.'"

Then I looked him in the eye. "Elvis, when I go this year," I said, "I'm going to say, 'Thank You, Jesus, for what You've done for Rex Humbard,' and then I'm going to say, 'Thank You, Lord, for what You've done for Elvis.'"

Elvis began to weep again, tears flowing down his cheeks. Maude Aimee and I grasped his hands and we prayed again. But in a moment, someone cracked the door a bit with the inevitable call: "Almost show time, Elvis."

As we turned to go, Elvis was pulling himself together. He said one thing more: "You and Maude Aimee coming here today and praying with me is the most wonderful Christmas present that Elvis Presley has ever received, and I want to thank you."

Steve Beard of *Risen* magazine would later write that Maude Aimee went directly to the hotel gift shop to purchase a tiny bell. During the second show of the evening, Elvis held it up and dedicated a song to her: "How Great Thou Art." Rick Stanley, Elvis's stepbrother, claimed that "Elvis recommitted his life to Jesus Christ on that night."

* * *

Elvis later invited me to Graceland. J. D. Sumner told me I was the only minister he had ever invited. Practically everybody who came in contact with him wanted something from him, and I hadn't asked for a thing. I had just prayed for him. Elvis was grateful for that and was looking forward to seeing me again. But when the invitation came, my schedule wouldn't allow it, and I missed the chance.

I would never see him alive again.

* * *

When he died, his father called me.

"We know all about your visit with him," he said, "and I want you to speak at his funeral."

So we went to Memphis. I officiated at the funeral. I told the mourners the story of our time with Elvis. As I stood there, looking down at the casket, little Lisa Marie came by with her mother, Elvis's widow, Priscilla. Like any preacher at any funeral, I tried to comfort them as best I could.

In the procession to the burial ground, ours was the leading car, then Elvis's, and then a car carrying all the flowers. It was astonishing, in a heartbreaking way, to see the streets lined for miles with people standing in silence, shattered by sorrow over this icon's passing.

Finally we came to a crossroads. A monstrous motorcycle sat in the middle of the street, and on it a monstrous rider, sleeves cut off, covered with tattoos, a huge helmet on his head. As our car approached, he reached up and pulled his helmet off, placing it delicately over his heart, standing solemn and still as we drove by.

At the cemetery, the hillside was full of flowers sent by grieving fans from all over the world—more flowers than I had ever seen in one place at one time.

In the weeks and months after the funeral, I got calls from Africa, South America, Europe, everywhere, wanting me to talk about Elvis and his spiritual condition. Finally I called Elvis's father.

"You know that I didn't come back here and tell people on my television programs about being with Elvis," I said. "I didn't believe it would be right. But frankly, I don't know what to do with the press's calls. They want to know something about the funeral, why I was there and everything."

His voice was weary in answering.

"Rex, forget it," he said. "Just tell them everything that happened."

I still felt uneasy. In the months and years since then, I've had many invitations to appear on talk shows to talk about Elvis. But I've turned them all down. I didn't want to cash in on a funeral.

Uncomplicated Faith

For me, it was all about souls. I avoided debates. People often wanted me to use my pulpit to criticize those I disagreed with. On many occasions people came into my office with a mind to debate me on some doctrinal point. My response was always straightforward: You can believe anything you want, but how is it benefiting you? I'm going to believe what I believe, whatever I'm getting benefit from. I'm happy with what I believe; how about you?

When we taped a patriotic special with Roy Rogers at Cape

Canaveral, we asked him to invite the audience to close their eyes and pray. He looked puzzled for a moment. "Cowboys pray with their eyes open," he said simply. At that moment, I realized again that God looks at our hearts, not at what we present to the world!

A gentleman in Mansfield, Ohio, came to faith through our programs and established a routine of going into the woods to pray and read his Bible. One day he had what he considered to be a supernatural encounter with God—he fell to the ground and spoke in tongues. Elated, he headed to his Presbyterian church the next Sunday morning and asked the pastor if he could make a comment to the congregation at the end of the service. The pastor welcomed him, and the man proceeded to describe his experience in the woods. Soon after the service, the church board removed the man's name from the membership rolls and told him never to come through the door again.

The man came to see me. He told me everything and wanted to know what I thought. "What should I have done?" he asked.

"That was your experience, not theirs," I told him. "You should have kept your big mouth shut. If God wants to deal with you that way, that's between you and God. But when you go talking to other people and trying to make them do what *you* do, that's wrong. If you came to the Cathedral of Tomorrow and wanted to stand up and talk about your spiritual experience, I wouldn't let you. We talk about Jesus, and we pray with people, and we let people alone. If it benefits you, good. If it doesn't, then that's your business."

I stand by that position even today. If more ministers today spent less energy on doctrinal differences and more energy on the simple Gospel of Jesus Christ, they would lead more lost souls to faith. I'm not concerned about somebody's church membership or politics or any other factor. A person is a person with a soul, and based on the condition of that soul, that person is going to spend eternity in either heaven or hell. That's just how simple it really is. Argue with people, denounce people, and you generally do more harm than good. If you see a young child holding a knife, you don't grab it because you risk doing a lot of damage. It's much wiser to offer that child a piece of candy. People are like that. Offer them something better, and they'll drop the knife. Hope through Christ is something better! People will drop their old destructive way of life if they can see that something better is available. Even the great Jewish leader Rabbi Tannenbaum became a great friend of our ministry because of our no-criticism strategy. He loved us because we were committed simply to helping people.

Faith does not have to be complicated. People ask, where did God come from? Well, I don't know. I'm not going to try to tell people where God came from. I don't have to understand everything; in fact, I can't. Nobody can. I don't understand how my brain thinks of a word, my lips and tongue create it, I speak it through the air, it hits your eardrum, and you hear what I'm saying. I don't understand how that process works. I don't understand how I can look and see different colors. My eyes are hooked up to my brain in some way, and my brain reports to me what these colors are, but I don't understand the system. Many people say, "Because I don't understand God, I'm not going to believe." But I accept by faith that there is a God in much the same way that I accept the miracles of speech and vision. I accept by faith that God is telling the truth in His Word. I accept by faith that Jesus Christ is the Son of God. I accept by faith that He died for me on Calvary's tree. When I come to Him repenting as the Bible has said and ask Him to come into my heart, He'll send His Spirit. That's what we call being "born again." I accept by faith that after this decision on my part, I'll be able to understand spiritual things, because God said spiritual things are spiritually discerned.

It's by faith that we get all these benefits. If, however, you don't understand how speech happens, you're not going to quit talking. Just because you don't understand how vision works doesn't mean you're going to quit seeing. Likewise, just because you don't understand God's work doesn't mean you can't be intelligent and think and use your mind, but you can accept by faith the things of God. And when you do, you're going to benefit. This is the simple truth about faith that I've taught for two-thirds of a century.

DEBATING HUGH HEFNER

For all my avoidance of debates, I must admit to participating in just one.

Talk show host Merv Griffin was assembling a program called "What's Wrong with America." He invited me, along with the chief of police, the president of NBC, film director Sam Peckinpah, and Playboy's Hugh Hefner. Well, this was an opportunity to reach people outside the usual boundaries, wasn't it! So I accepted.

As I waited in the green room before the show, the door suddenly opened, and several Playboy bunnies suddenly bounced in, followed, of course, by Hefner. Cameras were flashing. Hefner came straight to me and gave me a big hug, and I had a moment of panic: "Oh Lord, I'm going to show up in *Playboy* magazine!"

"Rex, I've watched you many times on television," Hefner said with a huge smile. "My parents are old-fashioned Methodists. They live in Chicago and they watch your program. They're great Christians!"

Sam Peckinpah wasn't as excited to see me. He'd had a few drinks in the green room, and he gravitated between sullen and surly. His language was foul. At the mention of God, he snorted—he didn't believe there was any such thing as a God.

"I'm going to prove to you that there is a God," I said, and he laughed.

I held up my little finger and wiggled it.

"Now you cut that little finger off and throw it away," I said, "and tell

197

every educator, every doctor, everybody you can think of, to put it back and hook it up to my brain so that when I want to move it I can move it. They might put a stub of some kind on there, but they can't hook it up to my brain. That tells me there's a higher power than man."

Sam wouldn't buy it.

Pat Weaver, the president of NBC, came in. How often was I going to get a chance like this? I cornered him.

"Mr. Weaver, before we get started," I said, "I'd like to ask you a question."

"What's that, Rex?" he replied.

"I want to know why NBC, CBS, and ABC will not sell me one minute's time—not even a spot announcement, let alone a program."

He looked at me in silence.

"Not only the network," I continued. "The individual stations that you own will not sell me time."

Finally he gave me a simple, true answer: "I don't know why," he said. "But it's true. None of the three networks will sell time to religion."

We finally walked to the set, the cameras rolled, and "What's Wrong with America" got under way. Merv had filled the audience with college students. The chief of police talked about crime but didn't say what caused it or how to correct it. Hefner, Peckinpah, and Weaver had their say. Finally it came to me.

"Man has a mind; he's not all mental," I said. "And he has a body, but he's not all physical. And he has a spirit, but he's not all spiritual. He is mental, physical, and spiritual. He has three dimensions.

"Man has progressed in the mental. We have a lot of knowledge. We could put a man in outer space. But when that man came back to earth and climbed out of that capsule, he found himself in a world where men hadn't learned how to get along with their wives, let alone the rest of the world, because something was missing. With all our mental advances, people can't get along, so we have strife, murder, wars—all these tragedies.

"In the physical, surgeons can do amazing things on the operating table. Medicine has made great strides. If I fall down on this stage and break my arm, I'll get the best bone specialist in town, and he'll be able to put the bones back in place, but he can't make them knit unless God Almighty makes them knit.

"In spite of all our mental and physical advances, you've still got a problem because you have not dealt with the most basic thing, which is the spiritual. Man is spiritual as well as mental and physical, and we haven't balanced. We don't have a moral base for our education. We don't have a moral base for our physical condition.

"What's wrong with America," I concluded, "is that people have left God out of their program.

"What's wrong with America," I concluded, "is that people have left God out of their program."

The college students jumped to their feet, applauding and yelling with approval. It seems that, of all the views offered by Merv's guests that day, the simple truth about God's design of human beings made the most sense and offered the most hope.

TEN

"Into All the World"

At the zenith of our television ministry, we were ministering on 658 television stations around the world. We had 800 people on our staff. Counting our programs fed via shortwave through the Far East Broadcasting Company, we were presenting the message of Christ in ninety-one languages. To conduct a crusade overseas in countries without adequate technology, we needed a 707 airliner carrying sixty-one tons of equipment. With different power systems in different countries, we had to carry our own generators, lighting, sound equipment, cameras, and more. The brilliant Bob Anderson, now a television industry legend, joined our ministry staff as a young, eager TV producer in 1974. Under his growing leadership, we engineered huge cargo containers to package our equipment securely and efficiently for international transport. For the sake of souls, we invented whatever needed to be invented. We didn't know the meaning of the term *limits*. We routinely went beyond the limits because we believed God, we trusted His power, and we were sold out, utterly passionate, about evangelism.

For a couple years, Bob stopped taking the mail at his house—everything went to a post office box—because he was on the road more than he was home!

People think of television ministry as glamorous, but my family and our ministry staff paid a serious price for the sake of the Gospel. On multicity tours across North America, we brought all the kids with their schoolbooks. They were taught by a tutor as we traveled—in an airplane, or in a car, or in a hotel room, or in the corner of a makeup room, or a dressing room, or on a stage—from city to city. They were always in the swirl of setting up the stage, camera, and lights; moving grand pianos and organs; and arranging speakers and lighting trees and cables. It took a crew of about forty-five people and two semi-trucks. It was a huge job just to keep the wardrobe, the music, the equipment, and the supplies all together! Yet they bravely and faithfully ministered in city after city, month after month—all the way down to my two-year-old grandson, Michael.

Television production is sometimes more chaos than anything else. Taping a TV special with Pat Boone, we needed a location that could double as the desolate hills of Judea, void of power lines or roads. We settled on a site in California's Mohave Desert. Moving people and equipment using a single helicopter required a couple trips, so for a time, Pat was left alone in a barren place. As soon as possible, the crew sent the helicopter back to him. Moments later, they heard the boom of an explosion, and looked toward the place where they had left Pat. There on the horizon was an ominous puff of smoke. They were sick to think that the helicopter might have crashed and Pat Boone could be dead.

In another second, however, the helicopter appeared in the air, heading toward them with Pat on board. Another boom and puff of smoke followed, and then another and another. They soon discovered why. The site they had chosen for their video shoot was the artillery practice area for Edwards Air Force Base!

Flying home from one overseas shoot, we landed our plane for refueling in the middle of an ice storm in the Azores, only to discover that the airport wouldn't recognize our American credit card. We had to pass the hat among our family and staff to get enough cash to buy fuel and fly home.

On a video shoot in Israel, we hired a shepherd, complete with sheep and camels, for the background of a Bethlehem scene. In the middle of the shoot, the shepherd suddenly decided he had to take the sheep away for watering. When the floor director objected, the shepherd drew a knife and threatened to kill him. The shepherd was promptly excused, and another flock of sheep was sought out and hired as replacements!

For a patriotic special, we scheduled a video shoot at the Statue of Liberty, but there was so much fog, Lady Liberty's lamp was invisible. We returned the next day. We had arranged for five hundred white birds to be released from the pinnacle of the statue. On cue, the birds were released, but we had the wrong batch of birds. These were pigeons with clipped wings. All but three fell to their doom—only three lucky ones made it to New Jersey.

Yet this turned out to be the single most popular television special we ever produced!

In the San Diego Zoo, a famous tropical bird—which the zoo staff assured us could not fly—flew away during our shoot. In Providence, Rhode Island, the stage access door was seventeen feet above the street, so our multiple tons of equipment had to be walked in through the front door.

In a winter storm in Minot, North Dakota, we had to hire a yellow school bus in the middle of the night to get to the local hotel.

Even when we ministered from our home base in the Cathedral of Tomorrow, our three generations worked hard. For years, our program opened with the two little ones, Michael and Susan, coming out first, standing in the middle of the stage and singing "You Are Loved," with the other members of the family gradually filling in around them. Our director taped an X on the floor where Michael was supposed to stand, and another for Susan. One Sunday morning they walked out—Susan in a nice little white dress, Michael in a suit and tie—and Michael noticed that Susan wasn't on her mark. So he pushed her, which she resisted. Determined to have his way, he lifted his microphone and clobbered her right on the nose. Gushing blood, she began yelping and running for Mommy.

The TV crew, rolling video, assumed we would edit out the accident, but I told them to leave it. That program, complete with the clobbering, was broadcast all over the world. We got letters from all kinds of places, saying, "We're so glad to see that your grandkids are just like our grandkids!"

Come to think of it, Michael was a burr in our saddle more than once. We were taping a patriotic special with Roy Rogers and Dale Evans outdoors on a hillside on a terribly hot day. Susan sat on a little pony while Michael stood there holding the reins. Dale sang a song, then Roy sang a song, then everyone sang "Happy Trails" together. Roy finished with "The Cowboy's Prayer." In the middle of the song, Roy quoted a poem. It all took an excruciatingly long time to tape, and when it was all over, Michael made an announcement: "I ain't a Humbard! And I ain't gonna sing no more!"

Through it all—through chaos, madness, and insanity—God was able to work. Our programs came together, were beamed around the world, and God used them to lead people to Christ.

Greg Diamond, a man in his late twenties with an accounting degree, was the vice president of a bank in Kansas. He had financial success; he had married his college sweetheart, a cheerleader. They had a life of adventure. They had dabbled in alcohol and drugs but were ostensibly successful. But one Sunday morning he woke up despondent because he had everything in the world except happiness. He sat in front of the TV in his underwear watching our program and prayed the sinner's prayer with me.

Long afterward when Greg shared his story with us, we looked up the date of the program that God had used to lead him to faith. We had recorded that program in Toledo, Ohio, one of the most painful video-taping experiences we'd ever had. We had recorded the night before in Detroit, and after a very late wrap-up, we had driven to Toledo to start at 7:00 a.m. Someone had substituted our equipment trucks, and the new ones were too small. Our crew had brought in extra equipment to patch together the production. During the setup at Toledo's Masonic Temple Auditorium, the tripod under the balcony camera failed; it fell over nose down to the floor below, and the lenses were smashed. With the setup such a disaster, we weren't able to have rehearsals. The crew was exhausted. The rally seemed doomed to be a failure in every respect. Yet *that* was the program that God used to reach Greg Diamond at his point of need!

"Don't Hit Them!"

My friend Paul Bruton, a missionary in East Africa for more than forty years, pleaded with me to bring our programs to Nairobi, Kenya. We did, airing on the Voice of Kenya television station, and we prepared to go into the huge Kamakunji Park with an open-air rally. We printed our literature in English and Swahili and coordinated our work with a number of area missionaries.

And people began to gather.

Standing on our stage in the middle of that vast park, there was a sea of faces as far as I could see. Thousands thronged to hear God's Word. There were people out on tree limbs. It was a stretch of humanity more vast than anything I had ever witnessed.

At the end of my message, as always, I gave the invitation and offered our salvation booklet, *Your New Life*. People began running toward the stage, hundreds upon hundreds of them, almost trampling each other. Policemen had been standing by throughout the event, and now they moved to the front with their nightsticks to keep the crowd from literally pushing the stage over. Some of the officers began hitting people, and Maude Aimee raced to confront them.

"Don't you hit them with those sticks!" she shouted. "They want this book, and they want Rex to pray for them!"

The policemen tried to argue with her, but they didn't know what they were up against. I've never seen Maude Aimee lose an argument!

I was finally able to pray, and thousands of Africans came to faith in Christ that day.

A Man Called Sin

We also had the privilege of taking the Gospel into the Philippines. Translation was not a major issue because English is spoken by most of the population. We simply translated our literature into Tagalog, the second major language. But the Philippines were predominantly Catholic, and no religious program had ever aired on Filipino television. As a result, the response was powerful.

At that time, President Ferdinand Marcos was still ruling the country. One day a meeting with his cabinet was interrupted by a call from his mother.

"You shouldn't disturb me during a cabinet meeting," he said.

"I don't care what you're doing," his mother replied. "I want you to leave that meeting and go turn on the TV to channel 7."

"Why?" he asked.

"Don't ask me," she said, "this is your mother talking to you. You go turn it on."

President Marcos, the powerful dictator, single-handedly governing the entire nation, could not disobey his mother. He left the meeting. He turned on his television set. There he saw, for the first time, the Rex Humbard Ministry program.

God spoke to the president's heart, and soon he was reaching out to me personally. We also became acquainted with his wife, Imelda, who greatly loved our ministry. She graciously invited me to speak at Manila's Kiwanis Club (the world's largest), along with Cardinal Jaime Sin, the highest-ranking Catholic in the country. There were more than a thousand businessmen in attendance.

I told them, "I never thought until today that the Lord wanted me to have fellowship with Sin."

Cardinal Sin laughed heartily.

He was an enthusiastic supporter of our work in his country.

"If the apostle Paul were alive today," Cardinal Sin told the Kiwanis crowd, "he would do his evangelism like Rex Humbard, through television."

He told me that our programs were leading thousands of young people to go to church in his country. "You've prayed with them on television to receive the Lord," he said, "and then you say, 'Go to church,' so our Catholic churches are prospering!

Our rallies in the Philippines were tremendously successful. The first was in the Folk Arts Theater, which had been built under Imelda Marcos's direction in just seventy-seven days, to host the Miss Universe competition. The facility stood on a landfill in Manila Bay, and when we arrived, it had already sunk four feet three inches into the landfill. The ocean air had corroded much of the lighting. It was a technical disaster.

We contracted for the use of KBS television mobile trucks, who proudly advised us that they had bought new tubes for the cameras and new tape machines. But they failed to mention that they hadn't put the tubes into the cameras. It was practically a miracle that we were able to get the cameras assembled in time for the rally.

President Marcos had imposed martial law, and there was a strict curfew—no one could be on the streets after a certain hour—so our team was locked inside the Folk Arts Theater all night, setting up for the rally. In the middle of the night, as one of the lighting cues was being set, there was a power blackout. At that moment, one of the crewmen stepped off the stage in the dark and broke his leg in two places. Team members had to transport him through several government roadblocks to the hospital, but he served during the rally the next day wearing a cast, with his leg propped up by the switcher! Meanwhile, we had crew members who had not taken well to the Filipino food, creating another challenge. And yet, as the rally began, God began to move. Thousands came to Christ.

When we returned to the Philippines a few years later, we had to move into the massive Araneta Coliseum, the site of Frazier and Ali's "Thrilla in Manila" fight. Turnout was staggering, in spite of 110-degree heat. President Marcos assigned four hundred uniformed members of the Philippine navy to manage the crowds. Loudspeakers all around the exterior of the stadium were plugged into our sound system so that the throngs of people who were stuck outside could at least hear the rally. Araneta had 30,000 seats, and it was estimated that there were even more people outside than in. People were packed into the entrance ramps and all the way out the doors. God's Spirit moved in people's hearts, and thousands received Christ that day.

We also went into the Philippines' largest prison, New Bilibid—a sprawling facility, virtually an entire town—originally designed for fewer than 3,000 but now home to more than 6,000 prisoners. Death row alone held more than 400. A missionary named Olga Robertson had been instrumental in getting our programs into the prison, including death row. She held a weekly Sunday service inside maximum security. They began each week by watching our program; then, as our program drew to a close, "Mommy" Olga would pick up and continue the service with her congregation of convicts. We took our entire production team into the prison for a full day to tape special programs and found that some of the inmates were actually members of our Prayer Key Family!

It was this visit that inspired the writing of my book *Billy Wasn't There.* Billy Salar had been a death row inmate at New Bilibid. At birth he was named for the evangelist Billy Sunday, but he had descended into a violent life of crime and ended up sentenced to death for murder. He had come to Christ through Olga's ministry and had become a tremendous leader, a powerful witness, sharing Christ among the inmates on death row. But his execution date finally came. He was strapped into the electric chair; he recited Psalm 23, and they turned on the power.

No one claimed his body. They finally took him down to the bottom of a hill and put him in a pauper's grave.

When we arrived, I sat in the electric chair where Billy died—but Billy wasn't there. I walked down the hill; I stood at his grave. But Billy wasn't there either. I looked up, beyond the prison walls, into the clouds. "We know where Billy is," I told our television audience. "He's with our Lord."

The program we broadcast from New Bilibid made television history, receiving a Gold Award at the New York Film Festival—the first time ever for a Christian evangelism program to be recognized in that way. Yet even more important to me was the eternal outcome: that award-winning program led many to the Lord.

CROSSING THE BORDER

Taking our ministry into Canada was almost
more difficult than reaching the more exotic locations of the world. There was strong resistance to
the idea of a Christian television program in
Canada. Finally we bought time on a station in
Detroit that reached into a corner of Ontario.

> Taking our ministry into Canada was almost more difficult than reaching the more exotic locations of the world.

Eventually Ted Delaney, head of an independent Toronto station CFPO, invited me to meet
with him. One of Delaney's staff had attended
one of our rallies and was favorably impressed.

"You're strengthening families," Delaney said.
"And you're preaching a message that crosses denominational lines. I'm
Catholic, but even my priest likes you!"

So Delaney decided to sell us time. And because his was the lead station for a nationwide network, in a single day we were suddenly on the
air all across Canada!

After the Canadian people mounted their unique strategy of building
identical "Centennial Auditoriums" in all their major cities, we borrowed
money from the American Corporation and conducted rallies all across
the nation. There had been theological conflict in Canada's churches for
years, and just before we began our tour, there was a huge uproar over
some major churches excising certain songs—"The Old Rugged Cross,"
"Power in the Blood," and others—from their hymnals. A number of
church leaders had asked us to come in; they felt our nonsectarian Gospel
could bring healing. In city after city, we packed the Centennial
Auditoriums, turning multitudes away, and saw thousands upon thousands receive Jesus Christ as Lord and Savior!

"Nobody Here Wears Shoes"

Often, in my drive to reach more souls, stress was high. When God first spoke to my heart about taking our programs into Japan, even members of our ministry staff were hesitant. Christians accounted for less than one-half of 1 percent of Japan's population. And our ministry was already, as usual, under financial strain because of our constant effort to expand into new areas of the world. Still, we went ahead and negotiated to buy time on channel 12, one of the leading stations in the country.

In a meeting in my office, Wayne shook his head. "Doc, we're having a hard time paying the bills for the stations we've got," he said. "How are we going to go on in Japan? There aren't even any Christians there!"

So I told him the old story about the shoe company that had saturated the U.S. market and wanted to expand. They sent two young salesmen to Africa in hopes of finding a market for shoes. The pair got off the plane, went into the city, and were astonished to find everyone walking up and down the streets barefoot.

"Nobody here wears shoes," one of the salesmen said. "I'm going home."

"Nobody here wears shoes!" the other exclaimed. "I've never seen such a market in all my life!"

"Japan," I told Wayne, "needs a lot of shoes."

God blessed our risk taking. We went on the air. When we prepared to go in person and hold a rally, our main contact, an American missionary, urged us not to rent a big auditorium.

"No one will come," he said. "There are no Christians here."

"We're on television," I replied. "People will come."

We had translated *Your New Life*, the booklet we've given to new converts for many years, into Japanese. We also had the Gospel of John in Japanese. I ordered five thousand copies of each.

"Rex, you're crazy," the missionary said. "That's enough books to last through the millennium!"

"I don't care," I insisted. "You print five thousand."

The day of the rally arrived. The auditorium filled with people. More stood outside, unable to get in. At the end of my sermon I gave an invitation to receive Christ, and people filled the front, filled the aisles, filled the spaces around the walls. The missionary and a number of his team members were giving out books as people came forward, handing them out as fast as they could. When they ran out of books, the missionary could only jump up and down, wave his hands, and thank God for the way He was moving!

Through my interpreter, I spoke in very simple terms—the same terms I've used all over the world—explaining the plan of salvation and inviting people to repeat a prayer after me: "I believe Jesus is the Son of God, that He died on Calvary that I might have forgiveness of my sins. I accept him as my Savior…"

But then something happened. In spite of Japan's strong cultural taboo against crying, people all over the auditorium began to weep. God was moving by His Spirit so powerfully in their hearts that the emotions simply spilled forth.

When we finished praying, I held up a copy of the Japanese-language *Your New Life*.

"I want you to read this book," I told the new converts. "You need the Spirit of God on the inside so that the next time you have a chance to steal something, something inside of you will say, 'Don't do that,' and you won't steal. You begin to say a bad word that you shouldn't say, and you won't say it. I'm going to pray for you right now, and ask the Lord to put His Spirit in you, to help you do the right thing and live for the Lord."

I turned to my interpreter. "Tell them that you're not going to translate for me now," I said, "because the Lord knows what I'm saying."

I raised my hands and turned toward one side of the auditorium and started praying. Spontaneously, the entire crowd in that area began to weep. I moved to face the center of the room, and as I prayed, they, too, began crying. I moved to the other side and prayed, and they, too, cried. God was softening hearts, breaking through centuries of religious tradition, and giving new life.

Our ministry in Japan became one of the strongest components of our entire worldwide ministry. The same missionary who doubted our beginnings later thanked me for making his work so much easier. For decades, missionaries had gone door to door to share the Gospel, and the Japanese would shut them out. Now, people were open to discussing "the same Jesus that Rex Humbard talks about on television." In a land where Christian influence was almost nonexistent, a Christian program on television was a shock—thrilling, captivating. (We had such powerful responses over the years that eventually the viewers in Japan were able to sponsor our program in Australia!)

"I Came to Kill You"

Japan inspired one of our most unusual television specials. I brought together Mitsuo Fuchida, the Japanese officer who led the attack on Pearl Harbor (crying "Tora, Tora, Tora!"), and Jake DeShazer, the bombardier from "Doolittle's Raiders" who dropped the first bomb on Tokyo in World War II. DeShazer volunteered for the mission, knowing he wouldn't have enough fuel to return to safety. He crash landed in China and spent seven years in prison (another plane's occupants also crash landed and were beheaded upon discovery). In prison, DeShazer's only book was a Bible, and as a result of that experience, he became a

213

Christian. Freed to his homeland, he pursued ministerial training and became a minister. Eventually he returned to Japan and published a tract: "I came to try to kill you," it said, "but I have returned that you might have eternal life."

When General Douglas MacArthur ordered Fuchida to testify at war crimes trials, Fuchida returned to Tokyo, stepped off the train, and was handed this tract. On his way home after the trial, he read it and was fascinated by DeShazer's story. He eventually became a Christian, contacted DeShazer, and they became friends. The two men traveled extensively in Japan and the U.S. sharing their story.

On our television special, I sat between them. I explained that Jesus had come into both of their hearts and made them brothers. We joined hands and we prayed, thanking the Lord for His love—for His crucifixion, death, burial, and resurrection—and for the gift of eternal life!

FIND IT OR BUILD IT

All along my goal has been souls. The Rex Humbard Ministry never criticized one person on television. I never touched on politics. I never mentioned denominations. If it wasn't about reaching lost souls with the life-transforming Gospel of Jesus Christ, I wasn't interested. But if it *was* about souls, then I was passionately interested, no matter what the cost. Children didn't join their parents in performing Gospel music when we started, but we saw how this could reach more souls. People weren't preaching on the radio when I began preaching on the radio, but we saw how this could reach more souls. People weren't ministering under circus tents when we erected our Gospel Big Top. A domed church as big as the Cathedral of Tomorrow was considered impossible—until we built it. There was no such thing as a church service on nationwide television when we went on the air. There was no such thing as videotape, no such thing as satellite broadcasting, yet we could not live within such limits. For the sake of souls, we pressed ahead. Beyond the limits. More trips to the Cleveland station to plead with the manager? Fine. More days of prayer and fasting? Will do. A microwave link between two cities where none had ever existed? Okay.

We teamed up with RCA to perfect the "model #1 kinescope transfer" which, for the first time ever, allowed film to be used as a duplication syndication source for television. We hung six 10,000-watt klieg lights across the front of the Cathedral sanctuary in order to provide adequate lighting for television broadcasts, something that had never been done before. We were among the first users of videotape in the television industry. We set up hydraulic camera lifts to allow cameras to go at eye level with the stage and make the worship experience more intimate for viewers. It had never been done before. Our attitude toward evangelism was, if we need it, we'll find it—and if we can't find it, we'll build it.

TRANSLATION INSPIRATION

Foreign-language translation represented a massive investment of time, energy, talent, funding, and prayer. We recorded in Spanish, Italian, German, French, Swahili, Filipino Tagalog, and more. Bob Anderson and his team established the system. A transcript of my sermon and the other spoken parts of the program, with plenty of white space between each line of type, went to the translator for each language. Each syllable was marked. The translator wrote the words, in the new language, in the white space between the typewritten lines of English. The differences between languages were often complicated. A single sentence in English, for example, might take a whole paragraph's worth of time to say in Spanish. We wanted to synchronize the video of my speech to the audio of the foreign-language translation as much as possible, so Bob's team worked in excruciating detail—sometimes literally inching the tape along—to get the desired effect.

Casting was crucial too. We searched for foreign-language voice actors who could not only speak the parts of the various individuals—Maude Aimee, our family, our on-air guests, and me—but could also match our unique inflections according to the various cultures we would be broadcasting to. Translation of each service became a week-long process.

Then the programs were duplicated and converted to the different electronic standards of the world. The United States, with 60-cycle power, used a format called NTSC; but in places with British influence, with 50-cycle power, a format called Power B was required. Some countries had more exotic standards—Power M in Brazil, C-cam, Mexi-cam, and others. In those days, the best available medium was two-inch wide videotape; as a result, a single one-hour tape could weigh twenty-six pounds. The English-language audio would be stripped off and replaced with the appropriate language, the stereo would be remixed, the English-language graphics replaced, and a new master made. For each country, our team had to make sure that the local addresses and other location-specific details were accurate.

The result: we could wish you a merry Christmas in Akron, Ohio, and in Nairobi, Kenya, on the same Sunday morning.

GLOBAL GOSPEL GEAR

Our technical teams were wizards. We pioneered the use of CMX editing for controlling two-inch tape, before which, much video editing was accomplished by physically splicing tape under a magnifying glass! We pioneered the use of the Editech system, which controlled two video-editing units simultaneously. We were the first to use RCA's portable TKP45 cameras—ours were serial numbers 4 and 5—and we inaugurated them in East Africa on our outreach there in 1975. The first images were of an open field which quickly became flooded with people as multitudes gathered to hear the Gospel. I visited a young man of the Masai tribe who had come to Christ, then attended Bible school and began serving as the pastor of a local church in his African village.

In the days before everything got small—or invisible, as with wireless satellite technology—television equipment was huge, bulky, and heavy. Moving it around was something almost nobody did, and certainly nobody routinely carried TV operations around the world. Tubes and transistors were enormous, yet delicate. Not even the commercial television operations took large multicamera video operations around the world. But because we needed to, for the sake of reaching souls, our teams made it happen. At the time we began our major international outreach, a two-inch editing machine was the size of a side-by-side refrigerator/freezer. The cable was extremely heavy. But to reach the people of Chile, Japan, Australia, and Africa, our teams designed the packaging systems to transport it all. Our shipping "pods" were A-1 air cargo containers converted into eight-by-ten-foot production units. Exterior shipping doors could be added and removed for shipping by air, land, or sea. The units could then be placed in a row on a flatbed truck and become a complete "instant" production facility. RCA and other manufacturers actually featured our work in a full spread of their international magazine. We were able to set up a massive stadium crusade, with as many as seven cameras operating in the ministry event, in a new foreign city every three days. In 1978 in Brazil, our teams muscled "portable" quad tape machines—terribly heavy conventional tape machines to which we had affixed rugged handles—around Rio de Janeiro, the beach at Ipanema, and Sugar Loaf Mountain, and in the near-Amazon heat of Recife. We held a massive stadium service on a Sunday and broadcast it as a Portuguese-language television special all across Brazil the following Thursday—and we did this three weeks in a row!

The technicians at RCA were puzzled to learn that our tape machines were lasting two to three times longer than the same machines in other studios. They sent specialists to Akron to investigate and discovered the reason. We had a no-smoking policy. Smoke was accelerating the demise of the equipment in everyone else's studios! *RCA Magazine* actually ran an article about their findings.

The incredible feats of our production team made it possible for us to minister in enormous crusades all around the world. We held crusades in Australia, from Brisbane to the white sands of Perth, and from the magnificent Sydney Opera House (beautifully designed, but clumsy for television) to the industrial city of Melbourne, all the way to the island state of Tasmania. In Sydney, by the time the Opera House was full, there were still more people outside than in. We held a second service, but there were still people standing outside who had not yet gotten in. A third service was out of the question; we were exhausted and out of time. Finally, Rex Jr. went outside with a megaphone, talked and prayed with the remaining crowds, thanked them, and sent them home disappointed. The power of television!

When we went to the wealthy city-state of Monte Carlo on the Riviera, we broadcast from the same tower that Mussolini had used during World War II.

During our crusades in the Philippines, my son Don led a TV crew into Tala, one of the world's largest leper colonies, with over twenty thousand residents. The people were longtime viewers of our programs, but the tubes in their few television sets had failed. They had been listening to our programs without video for months, so we brought in new TV sets for them. What a thrill it was to find even the people with the most severe cases of leprosy—bedridden, hospitalized—full of hope, joining with us by television every week. In nation after nation—the Far East, Europe, all over South America, and beyond—we were the first to broadcast a Christian television program.

At home in the U.S., we held crusades at the great venues of North America: Carnegie Hall, Madison Square Garden, Mount Rushmore, Cape Canaveral. As we prepared for our meeting at "the Garden," featuring Johnny Cash and his wife, June Carter Cash, we arranged to promote the event on the huge lighted sign at Times Square. The sign had never been animated before, but our team engineered a matrix that would make the lights appear to move. Our message, beginning with our slogan "You Are Loved," was the first-ever animated message on the lights of Times Square!

Our Madison Square Garden crusade was to be televised from a revolving circular stage in the center of the arena, and the schedule was a killer. An ice hockey game was scheduled for Saturday night, a basketball game would be played on the court Sunday night. Our event was between the two, on Sunday afternoon! And the Garden was notorious because of its unusual limitations. Its loading ramp, for example, was too narrow for our trucks. Even the circus, when playing at the Garden, had to walk its elephants up the ramp. But our team, as always, pulled out the stops and made it happen. The moment the hockey game ended, we began a brutal all-nighter, bringing in the components of the stage, the equipment, the cameras, the lighting—getting it all set up on deadline, then producing the event, and then undoing everything in record time to allow the basketball game to get underway on schedule! End to end, it was a nonstop twenty-four-hour process. Union workers, with nothing to do while our crew did the entire setup, sat backstage playing cards but presented us a $123,000 bill for labor!

The crowd began surging in the moment the doors opened, and when the building was at two thousand over capacity, the New York City fire marshal closed the place down, locking thousands more outside. Among the losers were major New York area business leaders who had helped us promote the event to more than three hundred television stations across the nation. We had given them special passes so they could come in through the stage door, but by the time they arrived, Madison Square Garden was already under lockdown.

Yet for all the challenges, this event touched lives in a supernatural way. Johnny Cash made a powerful impact in that program. He had really had an experience with Christ, and he opened his heart, telling our audience without reservation what Jesus meant to him, how faith in Christ had changed his life. People watching that program gave their lives to God!

THE LAND WHERE JESUS LIVED

The Lord also led us to the Holy Land. We had visited many times, and in fact filmed a primitive TV special with a single 16mm camera in the midsixties. We returned in 1972 with early video equipment. A grip named Haji carried our 325-pound camera up a fragile wooden ladder to get a shot on Mount Calvary, and we set up two 1,100-pound video machines as makeshift control rooms. We produced four programs from the Garden Tomb, one of which included our first-ever Communion from the Holy Land.

I had a longing in my heart to broadcast a Christmas special that would take people to the places where Jesus walked: to Galilee and Gethsemane, to the hills of Judea and the walls of Jerusalem and the shores of the Mediterranean Sea. In 1976 we carried a single camera and our "portable" equipment in a small van with four or five technicians and began to record a television special, scene by scene. Over the course of several weeks of shooting, we were able to lay out the video pieces of the entire Christmas story, all the way through Calvary and the empty garden tomb. When I spoke in a certain location, a transcript of my words was transmitted over a briefcase-style communications device—a forerunner of the fax machine—to nine translators, who began feverishly working on translations in their own languages. Once shooting ended, our team worked continuously, twenty-four hours a day, editing for four solid days to assemble the special in time for worldwide broadcast. But they made the deadline, and in the television special we broadcast to the world the Christmas story via this new thing called "satellite" and were able to share sights that most of the world had never seen. The special was seen in Rome; it was seen all across Chile and Brazil. In Tokyo it was projected onto an enormous screen in the downtown square.

As the special began all around the world, Rex Jr. had a number of our overseas team members connected by a telephone conference call. The Australians were thrilled; others were delighted. John Sakurai, director of our Tokyo ministry, was so excited that he began jumping up and down and yelling in Japanese, until finally Rex Jr. interrupted and reminded him that he would have to speak English if he wanted to be understood!

It was the Gospel's first-ever multilanguage satellite broadcast, and in many parts of the world, it was the first international satellite broadcast of any kind. It took the world years to catch up. Live Aid, the much heralded global television project, didn't come till almost a full decade later.

THE PRESIDENT'S CANCER

God gave us an extraordinary opportunity to minister to the South American dictator Alfredo Stroessner, who had turned Paraguay into a haven for Nazi war criminals. We were able to place our Spanish-language programs on the air in that country, and Stroessner was intrigued by our ministry. As we prepared for the South American ministry tour in which we would visit Paraguay for the first time, I began to sense something strange in my spirit.

Something unusual is going to happen. But I didn't know what.

Something unusual will happen in Paraguay. For two weeks, until our departure from the U.S., this notion gnawed at me.

Once in the capital of Asunción, the president invited us to meet with him. Our entire family went to the presidential palace. Stroessner had been battling cancer and had an ugly growth on the side of his face.

After the formalities, I said to the president, "If you don't mind, I'd like to have a private conversation with you."

He promptly excused everybody, my own family members and his guards and aides. And we were alone.

I told him about the unusual sensation I had felt for the past two weeks, and I asked him if I could pray for him. He agreed, and I did.

We held the rally at the stadium, God blessed, and we headed out of Paraguay.

About three weeks later, I got a message in Akron. President Stroessner's cancer had mysteriously dried up and literally fallen off his face. He called the Paraguayan Congress together and told them the entire story: how the Humbards had come, how I had asked for a private meeting, how I had prayed for him, and how he had been healed.

"If I had ten Rex Humbards in this country," he declared, "we would change our whole country in a month!"

A Blonde in Brazil

God led us into Brazil, that sprawling Portuguese-speaking nation of South America. We were able to get on the national network so that our programs were seen all the way up the Amazon in all the major cities and out into the islands of the Pacific Ocean. With our family onstage, the family-oriented Brazilians were enchanted. And with a vast majority of the population comprised of nonattending Catholics, our programs filled a void.

222

For the Brazilians, our blonde daughter, Liz, was the star. She was invited to tour the country and spent three weeks there, even addressing the Brazilian Congress. She visited Baptist churches and Catholic churches. She was a spectacularly effective ambassador, and by the time she came home, ours was the most watched program in all of Brazil. Soon we were preparing for a series of televised rallies across the nation.

Much of what God helped us to accomplish was facilitated by a remarkable friend we found there. Fausto Rocha was the most popular news anchor on Brazilian television, with a full hour of airtime every weeknight. Fausto fell in love with our ministry and committed himself fully to us. When we toured the nation in massive rallies, Fausto traveled with us and appeared in the services, to the delight of our audiences.

We began our tour in Sao Paulo, the largest city in the country, in an 85,000-seat soccer stadium, and still turned people away. It was the first nonsoccer event ever allowed in the center of the Sao Paulo stadium. As I concluded the sermon and asked people to bow their heads in prayer with me, the power suddenly shut down throughout the stadium. The P.A. system was dead.

I fell to my knees, and I began to cry.

"Lord, I've got to pray with these people," I prayed.

Without power, there was no sound system and no way for them to hear my voice.

But in a moment, I heard something unexpected. From high up in the stadium, someone began to sing.

Glory, glory, hallelujah...

More voices joined in the darkness. *Glory, glory, hallelujah...*

The volume increased. Tens of thousands were singing, some in English, some in Portuguese: *Glory, glory, hallelujah...*

They sang the entire chorus. When it was done, they sang it again. *His truth is marching on!*

Then, in an instant, without warning, the lights burst back on. The power was up. We had sound!

Through my tears, I issued that invitation, and thousands received Christ!

GOALIE EVANGELISM

From there we went to Belo Horizonte, with a 110,000-seat stadium, and had to turn people away. It was in Belo that we met the wildly popular star goalie of the city's soccer team. He had come to Christ in a somewhat unusual way. During the soccer season, the team was required to stay in stadium housing each Saturday night until the Sunday game. The athletes had little to do but watch TV; the goalie had begun watching our programs, and he gave his heart to Christ as I prayed at the end of a program! He wrote to our Sao Paulo office requesting literature and began a Bible study for his teammates. Watching our weekly program became part of the team's weekly lock-in routine, with several others becoming Christians as well. During our rally, we called him out, dressed in his Belo team uniform, and the crowd went wild.

"When we play soccer in this stadium," he told the people in Portuguese, "sometimes we win, sometimes we lose. But I'm standing here today to ask you to join the team with me and Rex Humbard and his family, because we are on a team that will never lose!"

The people erupted again, and he ran off the field. It was the highlight of a fabulous day.

In that fractious religious culture, where Catholics, Pentecostals, and Evangelicals had refused to cooperate on anything, some 150 churches of all types had cooperated to produce the rally. In our Portuguese-language edition of *Your New Life*, we printed the names, addresses, and phone numbers of all of those churches. A Baptist minister spoke to me afterward. "I've never cooperated with a Catholic or a Pentecostal," he said. "But this shows me I was wrong."

"He's Found Our Messiah"

God really helped us when we went to Rio de Janeiro. More than three hundred churches were cooperating there. The top magazine in all of Brazil was owned by a Jewish man who watched our programs and tracked with our successes in other Brazilian cities. He ran a major photo feature just before our Rio date, showcasing our ministry and suggesting that the arena we had rented would be too small. The government contacted us. You can't use the arena, they said. We'll refund your rent. You're going to have too many people. Someone will get killed in the crush.

And they directed us to a breathtaking alternative; they would give us, free of charge, the largest stadium in the world: Maracaña, with two hundred thousand seats.

On rally day, traffic was deadlocked for five miles in every direction. The stadium was jammed. An Associated Press reporter would arrive after the rally, out of breath, having run five miles to get there. "I've got to get the story!" he pleaded. "I'll get fired if I don't get this story!"

As I asked people to pray to receive Christ, more than one hundred thousand people stood and prayed with me.

In that moment, a Baptist preacher glanced down the row in which he was seated. There was a Jewish acquaintance of his, standing. After the rally, the preacher went to his friend, who introduced his wife and ten children.

"What are you doing here?" the preacher asked.

"We've been watching Rex and the family on TV," the Jewish man replied, "and we think maybe he's found our Messiah."

The next Sunday morning, the Jewish couple looked through the

Portuguese-language *Your New Life* that we'd given them at Maracanã and found the Baptist preacher's church. The entire family went to the service.

"We've come to be part of this church," the man said, "and we're going to be with you whether you want us or not!"

God is good!

THE DAY I LEFT MY WIFE

Sometimes our technological abilities made it possible to do the impossible, and sometimes the cause of evangelism required painful decisions.

The day I left Maude Aimee was one of those times.

We were still in Brazil; we had come to the capital city of Brasilia. On the day of our service, eager crowds had torn down a fence outside the stadium and flooded into the facility. The place was full; we started the service two hours early. When the crowd finally evacuated, we held a second service and filled it a second time. With everything being translated phrase by phrase for the thousands attending, the services were long and demanding. We all worked hard all evening, and Maude Aimee was particularly exhausted.

The next morning we boarded our ministry's small plane for the return to our Brazilian headquarters in Sao Paulo. But as the plane started down the runway, Maude Aimee suddenly screamed.

She was having a heart attack.

I raced to the cockpit and got the pilot to stop the plane before we left the ground. An ambulance raced out and took Maude Aimee to the military hospital, the best in Brazil.

There, on an examination table, my wife died. A man came running out to me, crying, "Pray, pray, pray!" Inside the room, doctors pressed electric paddles against her chest and hit her with a bolt of electricity. The monitor flickered to life for a moment, then flatlined again. They hit her a second time, then a third time. In the United States, three attempts would have been the limit, but they hit her a fourth time, and then a fifth. Again and again, they shocked her system, trying to get her heart to start beating.

On the tenth hit, the monitor began beeping, and her heart kept going.

I was shocked. Our entire family was stunned. Maude Aimee's condition was extremely critical. I could think of nothing but getting her stable enough for the flight home and getting her into the care of American doctors.

But there was a wrinkle.

News of our astonishing evangelistic campaign in Brazil had spread across the South American continent, and inevitably reached Chile. We were broadcasting our Spanish-language programs in that country, but we had not planned any appearances there.

The leader of Chile's military government, however, had other ideas.

He sent a committee to visit me in Brazil. One of the visitors was the top general of that country, another represented the nation's churches, a third represented the Chilean press, and a fourth represented the nation's television networks. They had a message from the dictator: Please come to Chile and hold a crusade in the major stadium in Santiago, the capital. The stadium would be free. The president would order every city bus to be free of charge on the day of the meeting. And the churches would cooperate.

But it was a five thousand-mile trip from our Brazilian headquarters to Santiago. We were already scheduled to return to Ohio, and my wife was deathly ill.

"We have a 707," one of the committee members said. "We will send it over. Load your equipment. We will fly you all to Chile. After the meeting, we will fly you all back to Ohio—all expenses paid."

It was an astonishing offer! We'd reach millions of souls in Chile, tens of thousands in the stadium. What could I say?

* * *

Maude Aimee's condition was so precarious that I was the only person allowed to go in and see her, and then only for a couple minutes once an hour. Our children and grandchildren were huddled in the hallway, crying and praying and miserable.

The offer from the Chilean government weighed heavily on my heart. I asked God for wisdom. I looked at my wife's ashen face. Then I went back out into the hallway and tried to comfort my family.

Finally I called them all together. A decision had to be made, and it needed to be right.

Maude Aimee's brother and his wife had made the trip with us. I asked them to stay with Maude Aimee. The rest of us would go to Chile.

"We'll take care of God's work, and God will take care of us," I told the family.

With a lump in my throat, I got on the plane bound for Santiago. We were a somber group as the aircraft descended into Chile, but as we looked out the window, we saw more than three thousand people waiting for us, all of them waving white handkerchiefs.

We went to the massive stadium, we held our service, and over sixty-five thousand prayed the sinner's prayer with me.

God honored our decision, our trust in His care.

The Chileans prepared to fly our cargo back to Akron, as promised, and in the early morning hours after our stadium service, my family and I returned to Sao Paulo. Maude Aimee was stable enough to be moved. She was carried onto our plane, and we headed back to the United States. She was under medical treatment for the next six months. But she was tough. And that was nearly a quarter century ago. She's still tough. Maude Aimee is still singing, still praying, still serving God.

It was ironic, in a way, that a grave threat to our family would open the door to such a ministry in Chile, because it was the unique family ministry of our television programs that attracted General Pinochet to us. As he saw our multiple generations—our children and grandchildren united with us in proclaiming the Gospel—he sensed that this ministry could be healthy for his people. No religious broadcasting had been allowed before in Chile, but God used our family, our family image, to break through the barrier. It was the same unusual concept that had attracted big crowds in rural Arkansas decades earlier!

General Pinochet, Chile's leader, was so grateful for our ministry to his nation that he invited us to return. We would visit eleven cities, from the copper mining region of the extreme north to the southernmost tip of the continent near the Antarctic Circle. Under his orders, we would have 100 percent cooperation in each city from the press, the media, and the local government officials.

We had breakfast with Pinochet, and the general was charmed by Maude Aimee. She gave him a "You Are Loved" lapel pin, and he jokingly objected: "I don't like this pin," he told her. "It says you love somebody. I don't want you to love somebody. I want you to love me!" Maude Aimee, momentarily forgetting that we were surrounded by armed guards sworn to protect the General's life, gave him a whack on the shoulder!

The Stage-Manager God

God has given me great health throughout my life; I had never spent a night in the hospital until I was in my eighties. As the doctors fought to correct a stubborn infection in my blood, however, I had to spend a number of weeks in the hospital, being fed an intravenous antibiotic "cocktail" every six hours, around the clock. It was dreary business.

One day the phone rang beside my bed. The caller referred to me as "Rev. Humbard," and he introduced himself as Dr. Emmanuel. He was the doctor who had been mixing the high-powered antibiotics that had been going into my bloodstream for weeks.

I thanked him, but he explained that that wasn't why he was calling. He wanted to tell me a story.

Some twenty-six years before, he told me, he was a child in Liberia, West Africa. When we put our weekly television program on the air there, he and his entire family had made it a habit to watch "every Sunday evening from six to seven," he specified. Through our programs, he and his family members, one by one, came to faith in Christ.

"Then you came to Liberia for your crusade in the sports stadium," Dr. Emmanuel said. "My family and I were all sitting right there."

He had come of age, traveled to the U.S. for his education, and had become a medical doctor. Today, by God's wonderful "stage management," he was positioned as the physician tending to my needs.

"Every day, as I mix your antibiotics, I am praying," the doctor told me. "Lord, let this mixture help Rev. Humbard," he would pray. "But whatever this mixture cannot do, Lord, please do for him Yourself!"

This godly young man was now reaching out to me, as I had reached out to him in West Africa more than a quarter century before. The Lord was revealing, and He continues to reveal, the fruit of our lifetime of pioneering labor.

Within days of Dr. Emmanuel's phone call, my heart soaring with gratitude, I was walking out of that hospital, eager to lead more lost souls to Christ!

ELEVEN

The Next Wave

$\mathcal{I}$n the wake of our efforts, other ministers came to prominence through the media. I celebrated the advance of the Gospel, if not always each minister's tactics. I also had the joy of offering some measure of wisdom to a number of them along the way because of our many years of experience.

When Pat Robertson was beginning his television ministry, we held a rally in his area, and he invited us to appear on his live program. He had nothing but a single black-and-white camera, which would pan from him to his guest and back again. It was almost funny, it was so primitive, and yet people called continuously throughout the program asking for prayer. The show went on and on until Maude Aimee, exhausted, stepped out into the hallway. Jim and Tammy Bakker were children's ministers in those days; they had a Christian puppet show on the air, and Tammy happened to be standing there. "When is this program over?" Maude Aimee asked her wearily. "Oh, whenever the Lord wants it to be over!" was the cheerful reply. "Look, the Lord's not turning these lights on and off, y'all are!" Maude Aimee said crossly. "When are you going to turn them off?"

* * *

Demos Shakarian came to our studios to record the first program for his organization, the Full Gospel Businessmen's Fellowship International. Their team began with a script, but Demos, like me, couldn't read a script comfortably. They taped him again and again, but he couldn't bring life to the script. Finally Rex Jr., observing the scene, came to me privately and begged me to put Demos out of his misery. I went to the studio and offered a suggestion.

"Forget the script. Just introduce him and let him go."

I prayed with them and left. They forgot the script and let him go. Demos did a great job. After that, shooting was smooth, and the ministry flourished.

* * *

I befriended Jimmy Swaggart.

Visiting his ministry headquarters, I saw that Jimmy and the staff prayed over viewers' letters every day at noon before going to lunch. He asked me to stand with him on a landing at the top of a stairway so the staff could see us clearly, and before prayer he addressed his team.

"Rex Humbard is here today," he said, "and I want you to know that he's had a great influence on my life and my ministry. I was in Canton, Ohio, years ago, and saw Rex on television, and I said to God, 'I want to do that.' I went into a studio and started producing a weekly program. It was Rex who influenced me to take that first step."

I had never known this.

"Then one day I tuned in to Rex's program," Jimmy continued, "and he was broadcasting a rally from up in Canada someplace. I said to God, 'I've got to do that.' So I got out of the studio and started broadcasting our meetings. I owe a lot to Rex."

As he invited me to lead the staff in prayer, my heart was full of gratitude to God. In His grace, He had allowed our ministry to be multiplied in countless ways through countless other ministries. I realized that multitudes had been touched by God's love through ministries we inspired, including the ministry of Jimmy Swaggart.

His scandal broke my heart.

* * *

Dr. James Kennedy of Coral Ridge Presbyterian Church in Fort Lauderdale asked me to fly down and talk to his board about the power of television in ministry. I was also invited by Jess Moody of First Baptist in West Palm Beach to speak to his board, and they visited our studios. When Dr. Jerry Falwell wanted to expand his ministry in the days before satellite, he needed a lot of tape duplication, so we ran a phone line from Lynchburg into our studios to tape his church services, then made the duplicates and shipped them. If anyone wanted to go into TV for the cause of Christ, we were interested in helping. We counted it an honor.

* * *

Along the way, we also funneled dozens and dozens of talented, experienced workers into the secular television industry. A secretary in our offices who learned the ropes with us ended up as a top editor for a network in Los Angeles. Missionary Paul Bruton's son-in-law wound up serving in James Robison's television ministry. Our son Charley is with the Discovery Channel. Our daughter Elizabeth's husband is in top management at CNN. Our former staffers can be found at all the major networks, at Disney, working on Super Bowls, or serving in a wide variety of Christian organizations and churches. Technology considered commonplace today was virtually birthed in our ministry.

* * *

The National Religious Broadcasters honored us by asking us to produce a television rally as part of their annual convention, which in those days always happened in Washington, D.C. But I was interested only if we could open the rally to the public and call the lost to salvation. So the NRB leadership agreed. President Jimmy Carter was scheduled to speak to the group's twelve hundred members. As soon as he finished, the lights went out, the stage revolved, and the Humbard Family Singers came on. The doors opened, and the public began streaming in, and we launched into an evangelistic rally. I preached the Gospel and at the end gave an invitation. The front of the auditorium filled with people wanting to receive Christ. I prayed with them and then turned the stage back over to the stunned NRB leaders. In all their years of annual conventions, they had never seen anything like it!

But they survived and later inducted me into the NRB Hall of Fame. That day, according to tradition, I presented the keynote address. I preached the Gospel just like I always do, and at the end I called on the entire audience of religious broadcasters to stand for prayer. "There's not one of you here today—I don't care how religious you are—but what you've got something between you and your God that you need to get out of your heart," I said. "It might be hatred; it might be strife; it might be trouble with your wife; it might be sickness; it might be finances. Whatever it is, I'm going to pray for every one of you that God will take

234

it away from you." After the meeting, a preacher with a big smile on his face grabbed me. "Boy, if the National Religious Broadcasters ever needed anything, that was it!"

DIFFICULT DECISIONS

We were on television about twenty years before others really grasped the idea of putting church services on television. When they did, the world changed.

For the first twenty years of our television ministry, I never once mentioned finances on the air. If viewers wrote to me, I wrote them back and let them know that they could help us keep our programs on the air by giving. It was done through the mail, never on TV. I understood instinctively that fund raising on television would drive sinners—seekers—away from the Gospel message that I was so passionate about sharing.

Others, however, looked at television and saw fund-raising potential. They bought time, produced Christian programs, and filled the airwaves with fund-raising pitches to pay for the airtime they had purchased. The emphasis in Christian television became "Help the ministry" instead of "Help the viewer."

It was during the early 1980s that I first observed a serious drop-off in the number of people coming to Christ through our programs. People were not being helped as they had been. Fewer people tuned in to television, particularly during time slots when they could expect to find Christian programs on the air.

Christian television audiences shrank; our audiences shrank.

At the same time, the cost of airtime began climbing. Television station managers saw the financial potential in religious programming. Instead of avoiding Christian programs, they went looking for them. With dozens of Christian programmers vying for airtime, TV stations could sell to the highest bidders. Airtime budgets skyrocketed. Our North American airtime budget was $8 million a year. Overseas airtime was nearly $6 million, with no income from those viewers. In every letter we mailed to our viewers, we were pleading for money. I even caved in and reluctantly allowed some fund raising on the air.

But it wasn't enough. It seemed that every other Christian program was a pitch for funds, and any money being collected was being given to the guys who begged for it.

My family, ministry staff, and I had to make some hard decisions. How could we stand true to the mission to which God had called us without crashing financially?

Our first step was to adjust the length of our weekly television program from an hour to a half hour, somewhat less expensive to purchase. It would be virtually impossible to carve a standard Cathedral of Tomorrow church service into a half-hour television program, however, so we began in 1981 producing programs in a whole new format from the beautiful Callaway Gardens in Georgia.

It was also attractive, I confess, to put some distance between our ministry and the Akron *Beacon Journal*, which had given us grief for decades, implying that we were fraudulent in the face of every success we achieved.

Our programs continued to feature the Humbard Family Singers, we kept the Gospel music, and I continued to preach the Gospel. Over the years that followed, we produced more than 150 programs from that site and aired them worldwide, still leading many to Christ.

We left the local Cathedral of Tomorrow ministry in the hands of Wayne Jones, who stepped up to the role of senior pastor. To avoid any appearance of impropriety—and to short-circuit critics who might complain that we were complicating the local ministry by continuing to influence it from a distance—my family and I completely excused ourselves from ownership and oversight of the Cathedral. Within years, however, Wayne retired, and the subsequent leaders mismanaged the church badly, until we were invited to return and take charge. We arranged to sell the facilities to television preacher Ernest Angley, who had ministered across town for decades, and he has conducted an honorable work there ever since.

* * *

Still, even after the reduction to a thirty-minute format, the financial pressure was intense. We found that half-hour time slots were not dramatically less expensive than the one-hour slots had been, certainly nothing close to 50 percent cheaper. So many ministries had taken to the airwaves and so much money had to be raised in order to pay everybody's airtime costs that the Christian television marketplace became a kind of competition. Some stations had charged us $300 a week in years past and were now asking $3,000. In New York City, we paid $5,000 for thirty minutes on Sunday at 11:00 a.m. and another $5,000 for Sunday at 8:00 p.m. We reached a lot of people; we helped a lot of humanity; we got letters from people proving it. But the fund-raising burden was staggering. And the percentage of our audience comprised of sinners—spiritual seekers—the lost—kept decreasing. Television, once a novelty where a spiritually needy person might turn for help, had become branded in people's minds as a place where Christian organizations hustled for dollars. In the minds of sinners, our ministry would be guilty by association.

At one point we had a network of 8,000 churches across North America whose pastors had agreed to let us refer new converts to them. From time to time I would call a pastor on the list to confirm that people were coming into their churches as a result of our programs. On many occasions they didn't believe at first that it was really Rex Humbard on the phone; I often had to do some convincing!

My friend Charles Blair, pastor of a prominent church in Denver, called me every week to report how many new faces had shown up at his church on Sunday morning as a result of our programs. But one day I realized that Charles Blair hadn't called me in months. I phoned him to find out what the problem was.

"I haven't had any new people come into my church," he replied sadly. "Do you think sinners have stopped watching Christian TV because of all the fund raising?"

The day finally came after thirty-three years of weekly television ministry when I felt that the pioneering baton needed to be passed. A new kind of pioneering must be called for. God would use others in television in ways I couldn't understand or envision. God would use others via other media too: the local church, books, the Internet, and still other means as yet unknown to us today. One day in May 1985, I walked into the control room as Bob Anderson and Rex Jr. worked with our crew editing one of our programs and placed my hand on his shoulder.

"I think we ought to shut it all down," I said to him.

Getting Good Advice

We continued in ministry. The only component we deleted was the weekly television program. We continued to hold rallies; I preached the Gospel at every opportunity; we ministered through the printed page to tens of thousands of people. We still do!

But money has become an even more defining factor in Christian television since then. Even the most notorious moral scandals of the past generation have had financial underpinnings. The PTL debacle is an example.

Maude Aimee and I appeared on the *Praise the Lord* program quite often, because we recognized that they were reaching people. But when

Jim Bakker began selling lifelong lodging at the PTL complex, I knew it was going to mean trouble. On one visit, I got him by the shoulder, steered him into the kitchen, and backed him into a corner.

"Now Jim, I want you to look me right in the face and I want to talk to you," I said. "You're going to get in trouble for what you're doing. When you promise someone something, you have to have something to back it up. You have no way of backing up these sales. You've already sold every room you've got. You're selling the same room two and three times. The government's going to come in here on you."

He was unconcerned. "I'm getting good advice," he insisted. The mayor of Charlotte, he said, was his attorney. He explained the whole strategy to me, all of which I had heard before.

"You're using the whole program time raising money," I told him. "I don't even want to be on your program anymore unless I can pray with someone to get saved."

He nodded.

"You've still got to do something about raising all this money," I said.

"I've got to have it," he replied, "or we can't exist. What do you think I ought to do?"

"I'll tell you," I said. "You go to Washington, D.C., and find the meanest lawyer you can find and hire him. He'll straighten you out."

Jim didn't do it.

His empire collapsed.

"I'm Going Home"

Scrambling to keep the ministry alive and himself out of jail, Jim turned the organization over to Dr. Jerry Falwell and asked that I sit on the board. I reluctantly consented.

My ill feeling about debates extends to meetings where the parties are in conflict, and this was exactly that kind of situation. I came to the first board meeting with trepidation.

At the table sat Falwell, Sam Moore of Thomas Nelson Publishing, Richard Dortch, and a couple of others, including an attorney. The air was thick with tension.

I thought I'd try to lighten things up a bit.

"Dr. Falwell, did you ever hear the one about what happened when the Communists took over the United States government?" I asked in a big voice. "The first thing they said was, 'We've got to get rid of all these preachers.' So they lined us up in front of the firing squad and invited us to say our last words. So Oral Roberts said, 'Something good is going to happen to you!' And Rex Humbard said, 'You are loved!' And Jerry Falwell said, 'This is your last opportunity to buy my large-print Bible!'"

The room erupted in laughter, but Falwell didn't take too kindly to the story.

The meeting proceeded. At the end of it, with a number of issues still unresolved, I told Falwell that I would be holding rallies in Japan over the next couple weeks, but I could be reached by phone. I gave him my twenty-four-hour office number in Tokyo as well as the private number of our Japanese ministry director. I urged him to have someone call me with all board-related information. I wanted to be kept in the loop. He assured me it would happen.

I received no calls during my time in Japan. When I returned, I learned that Falwell had held a number of meetings in my absence: two in Nashville, two at Falwell's headquarters in Lynchburg, Virginia, and one in Charlotte.

At the next board meeting I attended, Falwell made an announcement. As he was flying over to Charlotte that day, he said, the Lord spoke to him and told him to take over the place. I felt uncomfortable with this claim.

240

I listened for an hour or so and finally suggested we take a fifteen-minute break.

"My hands are so dirty," I said sourly, "I'd like to wash them."

During the break I came to a decision. Rex Jr. was waiting for me out in the hall; I didn't warn him. Maude Aimee was at home; I didn't call her. When we gathered again, I made a statement.

"I'm getting old, and I'm not going to waste my time sitting around arguing with people," I told the board. "I'm going to use the time I have left winning souls. That's all I'm interested in. I'm not interested in all the rest of this stuff. I'm going to resign, and I'm going to leave. I'm not going to talk to the press or anybody else. I'm going home."

Falwell begged me not to go, but I did.

The rest, as they say, is history. The titans of Christian media wrangled and wrestled for control of PTL's assets. Jim Bakker went to prison. It was all ugly and counterproductive to the Gospel, but at least I wasn't investing in it. I was doing whatever I could during those months and years to lead lost souls to Jesus.

Shaping an Era

I was astonished just a few days before "Y2K" to pick up *U.S. News & World Report* and find my photograph inside. It was the magazine's "Man of the Century" special edition, and they had named "25 Americans Who Shaped the Modern Era." There I was, alongside such notables as musician Louis Armstrong, feminist Betty Friedan, the founder of McDonald's, and the inventor of air conditioning! In fact, I was the only religious figure included.

At our television program's peak, the magazine said, "20 million people worldwide tuned in weekly to hear Humbard's folksy admonition: 'What America needs is an old-fashioned, Holy Ghost, God-sent, soul-savin', devil-hatin' revival!'" Its conclusion: "Humbard's successors still attract nearly 5 million viewers each month."

We had pioneered. We had worked and prayed and worked some more. We had made a mark. All for souls!

TWELVE

The Great Ones

Three outstanding people have shaped my life and ministry and have stood by me as my greatest friends.

The first is Billy Graham. I first ministered with Billy at a Youth for Christ event in Seattle in 1947. The Humbard Family was holding a crusade in the area, but Saturday nights were not included in our ministry schedule. So on Saturday evenings we brought our instruments and ministered in music, with Billy preaching.

In fact, God gave us the honor of playing a small part in the founding of Billy's evangelistic ministry. At one point in the late 1940s, we Humbards were making our way up the West Coast, conducting meetings in Oregon, Washington, and British Columbia. We had acquired a three-thousand-seat crusade tent and used it everywhere we went, but as we prepared to head back east, we didn't want to transport it. God led us to a relatively new group—Christian Business Men's Fellowship International—based in Modesto, California, and headed by the father of Gospel singer Cliff Barrows. I arranged with the group to sell them the tent at a good price, and Wayne and I offered to bring it to Modesto and put it up. We erected it, drove the stakes, set up all the chairs, and strung the lights using a single-action device I had invented to simplify the process. It turned out that Billy Graham was coming in to preach the crusade, and it was during this campaign that Billy Graham, Cliff Barrows, and George Beverly Shea came together to organize the Billy Graham Evangelistic Association, one of the greatest soul-winning ministries in history.

When Billy was preparing to preach at the old Madison Square Garden in New York City in 1956, I took two trainloads of people from Akron to attend his opening night. A radio personality in those days sat in the lobby of a major nightclub interviewing celebrities as they came through, and he wanted some coverage of the Graham event at the Garden, but Billy was uncomfortable going into such a sinful place. "Well, I'll go!" I said, doing anything to reach people where they were, and I happily promoted my friend's ministry. The radio host surprised me, however. "I go home after midnight every weekend," he said, "and watch you on TV. I like what you do!"

Later, Billy came to the Rubber Bowl in Akron, and I arranged for our church to furnish over four hundred prayer counselors and ushers for the crusade. When he returned later to Cleveland, we put counselors and ushers on buses and served his ministry there.

So for fifty-seven years, Billy and Ruth Graham have been dear friends of ours. He has been an inspiration, with his stalwart dedication to evangelism and his resolute commitment to a proven style of ministry. But he has also been a loving brother in Christ. Maude Aimee and I have depended on Billy and Ruth down through the years, and they have never let us down.

* * *

Another outstanding man of God who has shaped my life and ministry is Oral Roberts. And I had the privilege of being used by God to shape his ministry too. I nudged Oral onto television!

I had loved him ever since he was instrumental in the healing of our son, and I saw him from time to time down through the years, as both our ministries developed. Oral focused on healing; I focused on salvation. I liked that balance. As I became excited about television, I urged him to move from radio to TV. But he was nervous about the criticism he would receive from televising a healing service.

> **Oral focused on healing; I focused on salvation. I liked that balance.**

At one point Oral brought his big tent to Akron, Ohio, and put it up at the Rubber Bowl, where we'd had our meetings some time before. I helped him, heading up his committee to sponsor the meetings. "We've got to televise this!" I insisted. We got a crew from NBC to come in with cameras and equipment. Oral was terrified. So before the crusade began, I contacted a federal judge in the area and offered to pay him to sit on the platform during the healing services, take notes, and certify everything that happened. Oral seemed to relax a bit with this plan.

And the plan worked so well that he began arranging to televise all of his meetings, hiring federal judges in each city to certify the healings!

Our friendship with Oral and Evelyn has only deepened through the years. More than once, when I heard he was under pressure, going through some battles, I went to the airport without fanfare, flew to Tulsa, knocked on his door, sat down and talked with him awhile, had a word of prayer with him, went back to the airport and flew home. Oral sometimes did the same thing for me. I thank God for him and for his ministry. We've had a loving friendship now for fifty-five years.

THE NEXT KATHRYN KUHLMAN

But I must honestly say that the greatest friend I've ever known in ministry is someone a full generation younger than me, born in a different country, with a different ethnic background, with a different religious background from mine. Toufik Benedictus Hinn, now known to the world simply as Benny Hinn, was born on the coast of Israel in the same year that we opened the Cathedral of Tomorrow. His mother was Armenian, his father Greek, and Benny's family was Orthodox. When he was a teenager, the family emigrated to Canada.

I first met Benny Hinn literally by accident. I was visiting my brother, who was living in Orlando at the time, when I heard about an airplane accident. An airplane carrying the minister Benny Hinn had run out of gas. Benny was banged up, but the pilot was in the hospital, badly injured.

"Let's go pray for him," I said to my brother.

We went to the hospital, prayed for the pilot, and then, curious to see this Benny Hinn in person, we went to the service he was holding that evening.

It was a defining moment. As I watched Benny onstage, it was as if I were watching someone from long ago: Kathryn Kuhlman! Years before, Benny had traveled by bus from his hometown of Toronto to see her in action in Pittsburgh, and her ministry of healing had made a major impression on Benny. Through her influence, he had surrendered his life completely to Christ and committed himself to praying for the sick. It was clear to me that God had given Benny a real gift and that he would be, in a way, the Kathryn Kuhlman of the next generation.

I met Benny that evening, and it began a deep and lasting friendship. He was pastoring a church in Orlando and frequently invited me to preach. In later years he went into full-time media ministry on the road, which made it possible for him to touch multitudes of lives across the United States, Canada, and literally around the world.

Over the years as I observed his ministry, I admit to offering some words of advice. He was ministering the Word of God faithfully, and he prayed for the sick honorably—from the stage, while people were still in their seats, only bringing them to the front to testify of God's work in their bodies—exactly the format Kathryn had consistently used. His meetings were huge; they often filled 15,000- and 20,000-seat facilities to overflowing. But I sensed that thousands of the people attending Benny's meetings were not Christians, and they needed to be saved. I urged him strongly to preach salvation, make altar calls, and lead people in the sinner's prayer.

Benny was reluctant. "My ministry is mostly about healing," he said.

My ministry, of course, was mostly about salvation, and this finally led Benny to make a surprising suggestion. He was typically holding Thursday night, Friday morning, and Friday evening services in his crusades; I could preach in the morning session, sharing God's plan of salvation and leading the lost to faith in Christ.

I saw this as an astonishing offer, because in my experience, leading ministers rarely if ever turned their pulpit over to other preachers. But I accepted, and the results were tremendous. I think Benny and his staff were surprised to see so many thousands of people streaming to the altars to accept Christ! There were indeed multitudes of non-Christians in Benny's services!

For years, Benny gave me the privilege of ministering in all of his crusades across the United States and Canada. In every service we saw a thousand or more people come forward for salvation. In a two-year span, I had the joy of praying the sinner's prayer with more than 33,000 people, explaining the plan of salvation, introducing them to their new life in Christ, urging them to get into God's Word and link up with a Bible-believing church and commit themselves to growing in faith.

Benny has also welcomed me onto his television programs repeatedly; he has launched a project which will capture the story of my life and ministry on video. He has already conducted hours of interviews with Oral Roberts and me for a history of modern ministry.

"Just Plow"

As Benny's ministry moved more and more overseas—some 4 million attending a total of three services in India, 6 million in the Philippines, 9 million or more in Nigeria, and on and on—he invited me to accompany him. But I sensed it was time for him to take wing alone.

"You preach salvation," I urged him. "You give the altar calls. God will help you."

He did. It was thrilling to see how God began to work.

Over the past fifteen years or more, Benny and I have grown closer and closer. Recognizing our pioneer efforts of the past century, he has frequently introduced me to his audiences and explained, for the sake of many youngsters who cannot fathom life before television, how we blazed the trail for the cause of Christ, more or less inventing media evangelism as we went!

After the late-night finish of his evening service, we have often retired to an area set with refreshments for those who have been involved in the day's ministry. We've spent many, many hours in this kind of setting, with Benny asking question after question of me: questions about ministry operation, about doctrine, about conflict resolution: Should I do this or not? Should I respond to this criticism or not? How should I handle this kind of situation? I've been happy to share some of what I've learned during the past soul-winning century, and I think it's a measure of Benny Hinn's wisdom that he asks the questions.

One evening Benny closed the door for privacy's sake and asked me

248

how I felt he should handle a serious situation that had been presented to him. Another minister had made a dreadful error, and a number of prominent Christian business people had approached Benny, asking him to spearhead an effort to expose and bring down this individual before he could do any damage to himself and to the work of God.

"Should I do it, Rex?" Benny asked me. It was evident to me that he was deeply torn.

"When Jesus was dying on the cross," I replied, "with nails driven into His hands and feet, He looked down at the ones who had driven the nails and said, 'Father, forgive them, for they know not what they do.' We've got to get our eyes off of what we see, what we hear, what we read in the papers, and focus on one single purpose: winning people to Jesus Christ. That's the only thing you ought to be worrying about."

I thought back to my early days in Akron, with Dallas Billington raging against me on the radio. I told Benny about the horse-drawn plow we had used when I was young, and the blinders we put on the horse to keep him from turning aside and eating the corn instead of plowing the field.

"Put blinders on," I told Benny. "Ignore those who criticize you, and ignore those who want you to criticize others. You're about getting people saved and healed. That's your ministry. That's what it is. Look straight down the row. Don't look to the right or the left. Just *plow*."

This advice, simple as it is, made a big impression on Benny, and he has done well sticking by it over the years.

Today Benny Hinn preaches salvation brilliantly, gives a wonderful altar call, and prays the sinner's prayer with thousands. And *then* he preaches and prays for healing! I see in this

> Today Benny Hinn preaches salvation brilliantly, gives a wonderful altar call, and prays the sinner's prayer with thousands.

outstanding man of God a number of "streams" flowing together. He is the synthesis of Billy Graham the evangelist and Oral Roberts the healer. He is the combination of Rex Humbard the evangelist and Kathryn Kuhlman the healer. He is equally and strongly committed to meeting people's needs in this life and for eternity! I am proud to claim him as one who is carrying on our work, in the same spirit of single-minded devotion to the cause of Christ.

EPILOGUE

Today and Tomorrow

Today, I have to pick and choose carefully between requests for ministry appearances. Some of the ministries I helped to launch decades ago are inviting me back for twentieth and twenty-fifth and thirtieth anniversaries. Other new ministries are asking for help. I am constantly climbing on and off of airplanes, walking into studios and auditoriums and churches, preaching Jesus and calling people to trust Him and leading them in the sinner's prayer. It is a rich and wonderful life!

I am more about what is happening now and what will happen tomorrow than I am about what has happened in the past, and yet the past has great value. In recent years, some have expressed a strong interest in restoring and rebroadcasting some of our old television programs. Even secular venues find that our programs from the 1970s and 1980s have audience appeal. In many ways, they discover, our programs back then are better than many television programs being produced today. They're more wholesome; they have no vulgarity; they're entertaining. Like *The Lawrence Welk Show*, they have renewed popularity potential.

But no matter where I go, when I'm asked to preach in a church or appear on a Christian program, my appeal to people is the same: If you were to meet God today, are you sure you're ready? Is there anything in your life—a doubt, a fear, a sin, a habit, anything at all—you'd like to get rid of? You can do it through faith by prayer. You can be ready to meet the Lord and not have to worry about anything in your life that might keep you from being ready.

That kind of description includes a lot of people: people who would call themselves sinners and people who would call themselves believers. It includes church members as well as people who've never been inside a church. The Gospel is for people, regardless of their religious background, regardless of their status. And I am for the Gospel. I'll keep sharing it till I draw my final breath.

* * *

Hardly a day goes by without someone approaching Maude Aimee or me at our home, now in Florida, or in our travels around the world to tell us how our ministry has made an impact in their life. They came to Christ, or their children found God, or a loved one was healed, or a friend was rescued from tragedy. For this, I thank God.

Once in a while, I channel surf on our TV set at home and come across my own face. Someone, somewhere, is broadcasting a rerun of one of our old programs. I have to smile. God just doesn't give up. He loves people so much, He will pull any trick He can in order to share His love!

I am still a member of the Prayer Key Family. I still fast every Wednesday. I still pray over every prayer request I receive in person or in writing or by phone. I still preach the simple, straightforward plan of salvation at every opportunity.

I am still all about one thing: winning lost souls to Jesus Christ.

Crowd-filled
Humbard Family
Gospel Big Top

Putting God on Main Street: the making of the Gospel Big Top

A harvest of souls.....a precious time.

The old Copley Theater, the first home of the
Akron Pastorship

Calvary Temple

The dream of evangelizing
through television become
a reality in 1953!

From the Humbard Family Gospel Big Top...

...to the Cathedral of Tomorrow

The Cathedral of Tomorrow: from a vision to a reality

Services in the beautiful Cathedral of Tomorrow

Easter service in the Cathedral of Tomorrow, 1958

Thousands came to Cathedral of Tomorrow to hear
Rex Humbard preach.

Televised services from the Cathedral of Tomorrow

Rex Humbard prays as people answer the alter call.

Oral Roberts confers an honorary
Doctor of Humane Letters degree
on Rex Humbard at Oral Roberts
University in May 1973.

Rex Humbard
and Billy Graham

Rex and Maude Aimee
Humbard, Evelyn and O
Roberts, and Benny Hinr

Rex Humbard and Benny Hinn—two champions of the faith—share a heartfelt connection on a miracle crusade stage.

The Humbard family: (l. to r.) Don and Rex Jr., Maude Aimee and Rex, Charley and Liz

The Rex Humbard Family Singers at Calloway Gardens

Partners and friends of the Rex Humbard TV
ministry launch the Prayer Key Family in 1974.

Rev. Alpha E. Humbard

Martha Humbard

The Humbard family: (l. to r.) Charley, Rex Jr., Maude Aimee, Rex, Elizabeth, and Don

Rex and Maude Aimee Humbard

Rex Humbard Jr. Family

Rex Jr. and Suzy Humbard with
their grandson Shane

Michael Humbard

illyann Rosacker, granddaughter of Rex Jr.

Suzanna and Patrick Rosacker

Michelle and Rex III with children, Jeremy, Olivia Rose, and Shane

Don Humbard Family

Don and Sue Humbard

Joe and Donna Korb with
children, Joey, Samantha,
and Charley

Missy and Jeff Peterson with
children, Jessie and Jake

Susan and Brett Moorhouse
with daughter, Willow

Elizabeth and Dan Darling with children, Danielle and Dallas

Charley and Jennifer Humbard with children, Dillan and Harrison